VB6 AND WMI

Using WbemScripting and Get

Richard Thomas Edwards

CONTENTS

The last thing I want to hear 5

Getting Started, Again 31

HOW WOULD YOU LIKE YOUR WMI?..33

A Full Async Example 36

A Full Sync Example..39

The Many ways to use your WMI skills and impress people................42

Working with ASP 43

    For Single Line Horizontal...44

    For Multi Line Horizontal...46

    For Single Line Vertical 47

    For Multi Line Vertical 49

ASPX Code...51

    For Single Line Horizontal 51

    For Multi Line Horizontal 53

For Single Line Vertical 55

For Multi Line Vertical 56

HTA Code 59

For Single Line Horizontal..59

For Multi Line Horizontal..61

For Single Line Vertical 63

For Multi Line Vertical 64

HTML Code 67

For Single Line Horizontal..67

For Multi Line Horizontal..69

For Single Line Vertical 70

For Multi Line Vertical 72

Text Delimited File Examples 74

Colon 74

Comma Delimited 76

Exclamation 77

SEMI COLON..79

Tab Delimited..80

Tilde Delimited..82

THE XML FILES..84

Element XML..84

WMI to Element XML For XSL 85

SCHEMA XML..85

EXCEL 87

Using the comma delimited file 87

Excel Automation 89

Using A Spreadsheet 91

XSL..95

SINGLE LINE HORIZONTAL...95

For Multi Line Horizontal 97

For Single Line Vertical...99

For Multi Line Vertical...100

Stylesheets...103

Stylesheets 109

NONE 109

BLACK AND WHITE TEXT 110

COLORED TEXT 112

OSCILLATING ROW COLORS 114

GHOST DECORATED 117

3D 119

SHADOW BOX..125

Appendix B 131

The last thing I want to hear

You know it left and is living in a retirement home, don't you?

NEVER GIVE UP, NEVER SURRUNDER! That's my reply. And with that said, this book is about using WbemScripting and the WbemScripting.SWbemServices' InstancesOf interface to create a lot of different outputs. It is one of many books using WbemScripting and using the exact same output examples. There will be books on showing you how to make use of WbemScripting in both sync and async modes.

Here's my suggestion, you can use anyone of the following three

I'm mentioning this so that if you do decide to use the references, you can do the following:

Early Binding:

Dim l as Wbemscripting.SWbemLocator

Dim svc as WbemScripting.SWbemServices

Dim objs as WbemScripting.SWbemObjectSet

Dim obj as WbemScripting.SWbemObject

Dim ob as WbemScripting.SWbemObject

Dim Propset as WbemScripting.SWbemPropertySet

```
Dim prop  as WbemScripting.SWbemProperty

Set l = new WbemScripting.SWbemLocator
Set svc = l.ConnectServer(".", "root\cimv2")
svc.Security_.AuthenticationLevel = 6
svc.Security_.ImpersonationLevel = 3
Set ob = svc.Get("Win32_Process")
Set objs = ob.Instances_
for each obj in objs
  for each prop in obj.Properties_
  next
Next

Function GetValue(ByVal Name, ByVal obj)

  Dim tempstr, pos, pName
  pName = Name
  tempstr = obj.GetObjectText_
  Name = Name + " = "
  pos = InStr(tempstr, Name)
  If pos Then

    pos = pos + Len(Name)
    tempstr = Mid(tempstr, pos, Len(tempstr))
    pos = InStr(tempstr, ";")
    tempstr = Mid(tempstr, 1, pos - 1)
    tempstr = Replace(tempstr, Chr(34), "")
    tempstr = Replace(tempstr, "{", "")
    tempstr = Replace(tempstr, "}", "")
    tempstr = Trim(tempstr)

    If obj.Properties_(pName).CIMType = 101 Then
```

```
        tempstr = Mid(tempstr, 5, 2) + "/" + _
                Mid(tempstr, 7, 2) + "/" + _
                Mid(tempstr, 1, 4) + " " + _
                Mid(tempstr, 9, 2) + ":" + _
                Mid(tempstr, 11, 2) + ":" + _
                Mid(tempstr, 13, 2)

    End If

    GetValue = tempstr

  Else

    GetValue = ""

  End If

End Function
```

Results:

```
Private Sub Form_Load()
Module1.Initialize
Me.Caption = "Win32_Proces"
Set ws = CreateObject("WScript.Shell")
WebBrowser1.Navigate (ws.CurrentDirectory + "\Win32_Process.html")
End Sub

Private Sub Form_Resize()
WebBrowser1.Top = Me.ScaleTop
WebBrowser1.Left = Me.ScaleLeft
WebBrowser1.Width = Me.ScaleWidth
WebBrowser1.Height = Me.ScaleHeight
End Sub
```

Win32_Proces

Caption	CommandLine
System Idle Process	
System	
smss.exe	
csrss.exe	
wininit.exe	wininit.exe
csrss.exe	
services.exe	
lsass.exe	C:\Windows\system32\lsass.exe
svchost.exe	C:\Windows\system32\svchost.exe -k DcomLaunch
winlogon.exe	winlogon.exe
svchost.exe	C:\Windows\system32\svchost.exe -k RPCSS
dwm.exe	\dwm.exe\
NVDisplay.Container.exe	C:\Program Files\NVIDIA Corporation\Display.NvContainer\NVDisplay.Container.exe
svchost.exe	C:\Windows\System32\svchost.exe -k LocalServiceNetworkRestricted
svchost.exe	C:\Windows\system32\svchost.exe -k netsvcs
svchost.exe	C:\Windows\system32\svchost.exe -k LocalService
svchost.exe	C:\Windows\system32\svchost.exe -k NetworkService
svchost.exe	C:\Windows\System32\svchost.exe -k LocalSystemNetworkRestricted
svchost.exe	C:\Windows\system32\svchost.exe -k LocalServiceNoNetwork
spoolsv.exe	C:\Windows\System32\spoolsv.exe
svchost.exe	C:\Windows\system32\svchost.exe -k apphost
OfficeClickToRun.exe	\C:\Program Files\Common Files\Microsoft Shared\ClickToRun\OfficeClickToRun.exe\
svchost.exe	C:\Windows\system32\svchost.exe -k ftpsvc
inetinfo.exe	C:\Windows\system32\inetsrv\inetinfo.exe
KindleDesktopService.exe	C:\Program Files (x86)\Amazon\KindleAddIn\Service\KindleDesktopService.exe\
NvTelemetryContainer.exe	C:\Program Files (x86)\NVIDIA Corporation\NvTelemetry\NvTelemetryContainer.exe\

Mixed Binding:

```
Dim l as Wbemscripting.SWbemLocator
Dim svc as WbemScripting.SWbemServices
Dim objs as WbemScripting.SWbemObjectSet
Dim obj as WbemScripting.SWbemObject
Dim ob as WbemScripting.SWbemObject
Dim Propset as SWbemScripting.SWbemPropertySet
Dim prop  as WbemScripting.SWbemProperty

Set l = CreateObject("WbemScripting.SWbemLocator")
Set svc = l.ConnectServer(".", "root\cimv2")
svc.Security_.AuthenticationLevel = 6
svc.Security_.ImpersonationLevel = 3
Set ob = svc.Get("Win32_Process")
Set objs = ob.Instances_
for each obj in objs
  for each prop in obj.Properties_
  next
next

Function GetValue(ByVal Name, ByVal obj)

  Dim tempstr, pos, pName
  pName = Name
  tempstr = obj.GetObjectText_
  Name = Name + " = "
  pos = InStr(tempstr, Name)
  If pos Then

    pos = pos + Len(Name)
    tempstr = Mid(tempstr, pos, Len(tempstr))
```

```vb
    pos = InStr(tempstr, ";")
    tempstr = Mid(tempstr, 1, pos - 1)
    tempstr = Replace(tempstr, Chr(34), "")
    tempstr = Replace(tempstr, "{", "")
    tempstr = Replace(tempstr, "}", "")
    tempstr = Trim(tempstr)

    If obj.Properties_(pName).CIMType = 101 Then

      tempstr = Mid(tempstr, 5, 2) + "/" + _
            Mid(tempstr, 7, 2) + "/" + _
            Mid(tempstr, 1, 4) + " " + _
            Mid(tempstr, 9, 2) + ":" + _
            Mid(tempstr, 11, 2) + ":" + _
            Mid(tempstr, 13, 2)

    End If

    GetValue = tempstr

  Else

    GetValue = ""

  End If

End Function
```

The results:

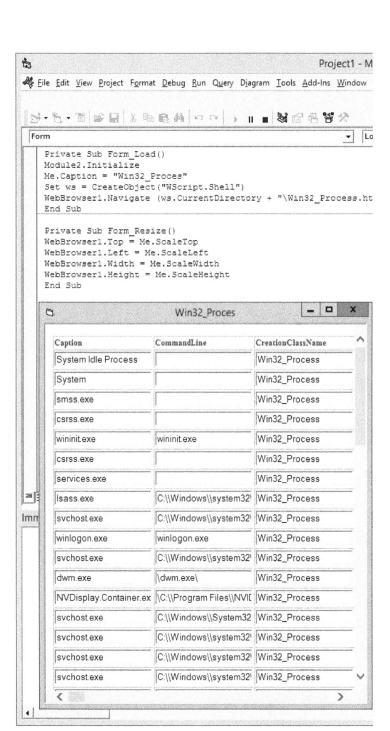

Late Binding:

```
Set l = CreateObject("WbemScripting.SWbemLocator")
Set svc = l.ConnectServer(".", "root\cimv2")
svc.Security_.AuthenticationLevel = 6
svc.Security_.ImpersonationLevel = 3
Set ob = svc.Get("Win32_Process")
Set objs = ob.Instances_
for each obj in objs
  for each prop in obj.Properties_
  next
next

Function GetValue(ByVal Name, ByVal obj)

  Dim tempstr, pos, pName
  pName = Name
  tempstr = obj.GetObjectText_
  Name = Name + " = "
  pos = InStr(tempstr, Name)
  If pos Then

    pos = pos + Len(Name)
    tempstr = Mid(tempstr, pos, Len(tempstr))
    pos = InStr(tempstr, ";")
    tempstr = Mid(tempstr, 1, pos - 1)
    tempstr = Replace(tempstr, Chr(34), "")
    tempstr = Replace(tempstr, "{", "")
    tempstr = Replace(tempstr, "}", "")
    tempstr = Trim(tempstr)

    If obj.Properties_(pName).CIMType = 101 Then
```

```
        tempstr = Mid(tempstr, 5, 2) + "/" + _
            Mid(tempstr, 7, 2) + "/" + _
            Mid(tempstr, 1, 4) + " " + _
            Mid(tempstr, 9, 2) + ":" + _
            Mid(tempstr, 11, 2) + ":" + _
            Mid(tempstr, 13, 2)

    End If

    GetValue = tempstr

  Else

    GetValue = ""

  End If

End Function
```

The first two examples will require a reference to the Microsoft WMI Scripting V1.2 Library. The last one, you don't.

Module1 code:

Public Sub Initialize()

```
Dim l As WbemScripting.SWbemLocator
Dim svc As WbemScripting.SWbemServices
Dim objs As WbemScripting.SWbemObjectSet
Dim obj As WbemScripting.SWbemObject
Dim ob As WbemScripting.SWbemObject
Dim Propset As WbemScripting.SWbemPropertySet
Dim prop  As WbemScripting.SWbemProperty

Set l = New WbemScripting.SWbemLocator
Set svc = l.ConnectServer(".", "root\cimv2")
svc.Security_.AuthenticationLevel = 6
svc.Security_.ImpersonationLevel = 3
Set ob = svc.Get("Win32_Process")
Set objs = ob.Instances_

Call Write_The_Output(objs)

End Sub


Public Sub Write_The_Output(ByVal objs As Object)

Set ws = CreateObject("WScript.Shell")
Set fso = CreateObject("Scripting.FileSystemObject")
```

```
Set txtstream = fso.OpenTextFile(ws.CurrentDirectory + "\Win32_Process.html", 2,
True, -2)
txtstream.WriteLine ("<html>")
txtstream.WriteLine ("<head>")
txtstream.WriteLine ("<style type='text/css'>")
txtstream.WriteLine ("th")
txtstream.WriteLine ("{")
txtstream.WriteLine ("    COLOR: darkred;")
txtstream.WriteLine ("    BACKGROUND-COLOR: white;")
txtstream.WriteLine ("    FONT-FAMILY:font-family: Cambria, serif;")
txtstream.WriteLine ("    FONT-SIZE: 12px;")
txtstream.WriteLine ("    text-align: left;")
txtstream.WriteLine ("    white-Space: nowrap;")
txtstream.WriteLine ("}")
txtstream.WriteLine ("td")
txtstream.WriteLine ("{")
txtstream.WriteLine ("    COLOR: navy;")
txtstream.WriteLine ("    BACKGROUND-COLOR: white;")
txtstream.WriteLine ("    FONT-FAMILY: font-family: Cambria, serif;")
txtstream.WriteLine ("    FONT-SIZE: 12px;")
txtstream.WriteLine ("    text-align: left;")
txtstream.WriteLine ("    white-Space: nowrap;")
txtstream.WriteLine ("}")
txtstream.WriteLine ("</style>")
txtstream.WriteLine ("<title>Win32_Process</title>")
txtstream.WriteLine ("</head>")
txtstream.WriteLine ("<body>")
txtstream.WriteLine ("<table Border='1' cellpadding='1' cellspacing='1'>")
Set obj = objs.ItemIndex(0)
txtstream.WriteLine ("<tr>")
For Each prop In obj.Properties_
    txtstream.WriteLine ("<th>" & prop.Name & "</th>")
Next
```

```
txtstream.WriteLine ("</tr>")
For Each obj In objs
   txtstream.WriteLine ("<tr>")
   For Each prop In obj.Properties_
      txtstream.WriteLine ("<td>" & GetValue(prop.Name, obj) & "</td>")
   Next
   txtstream.WriteLine ("</tr>")
Next
txtstream.WriteLine ("</table>")
txtstream.WriteLine ("</body>")
txtstream.WriteLine ("</html>")
txtstream.Close


End Sub


Function GetValue(ByVal Name, ByVal obj)

  Dim tempstr, pos, pName
  pName = Name
  tempstr = obj.GetObjectText_
  Name = Name + " = "
  pos = InStr(tempstr, Name)
  If pos Then

    pos = pos + Len(Name)
    tempstr = Mid(tempstr, pos, Len(tempstr))
    pos = InStr(tempstr, ";")
    tempstr = Mid(tempstr, 1, pos - 1)
    tempstr = Replace(tempstr, Chr(34), "")
    tempstr = Replace(tempstr, "{", "")
    tempstr = Replace(tempstr, "}", "")
```

```vba
    tempstr = Trim(tempstr)

    If obj.Properties_(pName).CIMType = 101 Then

      tempstr = Mid(tempstr, 5, 2) + "/" + _
          Mid(tempstr, 7, 2) + "/" + _
          Mid(tempstr, 1, 4) + " " + _
          Mid(tempstr, 9, 2) + ":" + _
          Mid(tempstr, 11, 2) + ":" + _
          Mid(tempstr, 13, 2)

    End If

    GetValue = tempstr

  Else

    GetValue = ""

  End If

End Function
```

Module 2 Code:

```vba
Public Sub Initialize()

Dim l As WbemScripting.SWbemLocator
Dim svc As WbemScripting.SWbemServices
Dim objs As WbemScripting.SWbemObjectSet
Dim obj As WbemScripting.SWbemObject
Dim ob As WbemScripting.SWbemObject
Dim Propset As WbemScripting.SWbemPropertySet
```

```vb
Dim prop  As WbemScripting.SWbemProperty

Set l = CreateObject("WbemScripting.SWbemLocator")
Set svc = l.ConnectServer(".", "root\cimv2")
svc.Security_.AuthenticationLevel = 6
svc.Security_.ImpersonationLevel = 3
Set ob = svc.Get("Win32_Process")
Set objs = ob.Instances_

Call Write_The_Output(objs)

End Sub


Public Sub Write_The_Output(ByVal objs As Object)

Set ws = CreateObject("WScript.Shell")
Set fso = CreateObject("Scripting.FileSystemObject")
Set txtstream = fso.OpenTextFile(ws.CurrentDirectory + "\Win32_Process.html", 2,
True, -2)
txtstream.WriteLine ("<html>")
txtstream.WriteLine ("<head>")
txtstream.WriteLine ("<style type='text/css'>")
txtstream.WriteLine ("th")
txtstream.WriteLine ("{")
txtstream.WriteLine ("    COLOR: darkred;")
txtstream.WriteLine ("    BACKGROUND-COLOR: white;")
txtstream.WriteLine ("    FONT-FAMILY:font-family: Cambria, serif;")
txtstream.WriteLine ("    FONT-SIZE: 12px;")
txtstream.WriteLine ("    text-align: left;")
txtstream.WriteLine ("    white-Space: nowrap;")
txtstream.WriteLine ("}")
txtstream.WriteLine ("td")
```

```
txtstream.WriteLine ("{")
txtstream.WriteLine ("   COLOR: navy;")
txtstream.WriteLine ("   BACKGROUND-COLOR: white;")
txtstream.WriteLine ("   FONT-FAMILY: font-family: Cambria, serif;")
txtstream.WriteLine ("   FONT-SIZE: 12px;")
txtstream.WriteLine ("   text-align: left;")
txtstream.WriteLine ("   white-Space: nowrap;")
txtstream.WriteLine ("}")
txtstream.WriteLine ("</style>")
txtstream.WriteLine ("<title>Win32_Process</title>")
txtstream.WriteLine ("</head>")
txtstream.WriteLine ("<body>")
txtstream.WriteLine ("<table Border='1' cellpadding='1' cellspacing='1'>")
Set obj = objs.ItemIndex(0)
txtstream.WriteLine ("<tr>")
For Each prop In obj.Properties_
   txtstream.WriteLine ("<th>" & prop.Name & "</th>")
Next
txtstream.WriteLine ("</tr>")
For Each obj In objs
   txtstream.WriteLine ("<tr>")
   For Each prop In obj.Properties_
      txtstream.WriteLine      ("<td><input      type=""text""      value=""""      &
GetValue(prop.Name, obj) & """"></input></td>")
   Next
   txtstream.WriteLine ("</tr>")
Next
txtstream.WriteLine ("</table>")
txtstream.WriteLine ("</body>")
txtstream.WriteLine ("</html>")
txtstream.Close
```

```
End Sub


Function GetValue(ByVal Name, ByVal obj)

 Dim tempstr, pos, pName
 pName = Name
 tempstr = obj.GetObjectText_
 Name = Name + " = "
 pos = InStr(tempstr, Name)
 If pos Then

   pos = pos + Len(Name)
   tempstr = Mid(tempstr, pos, Len(tempstr))
   pos = InStr(tempstr, ";")
   tempstr = Mid(tempstr, 1, pos - 1)
   tempstr = Replace(tempstr, Chr(34), "")
   tempstr = Replace(tempstr, "{", "")
   tempstr = Replace(tempstr, "}", "")
   tempstr = Trim(tempstr)

   If obj.Properties_(pName).CIMType = 101 Then

     tempstr = Mid(tempstr, 5, 2) + "/" + _
          Mid(tempstr, 7, 2) + "/" + _
          Mid(tempstr, 1, 4) + " " + _
          Mid(tempstr, 9, 2) + ":" + _
          Mid(tempstr, 11, 2) + ":" + _
          Mid(tempstr, 13, 2)

   End If

 GetValue = tempstr
```

```
        Else

           GetValue = ""

        End If

End Function

Module 3 Code:

Public Sub Initialize()


Set l = CreateObject("WbemScripting.SWbemLocator")
Set svc = l.ConnectServer(".", "root\cimv2")
svc.Security_.AuthenticationLevel = 6
svc.Security_.ImpersonationLevel = 3
Set ob = svc.Get("Win32_Process")
Set objs = ob.Instances_

Call Write_The_Output(objs)

End Sub


Public Sub Write_The_Output(ByVal objs As Object)

Set ws = CreateObject("WScript.Shell")
Set fso = CreateObject("Scripting.FileSystemObject")
Set txtstream = fso.OpenTextFile(ws.CurrentDirectory + "\Win32_Process.html", 2,
True, -2)
txtstream.WriteLine ("<html>")
```

```
txtstream.WriteLine ("<head>")
txtstream.WriteLine ("<style type='text/css'>")
txtstream.WriteLine ("body")
txtstream.WriteLine ("{")
txtstream.WriteLine ("    PADDING-RIGHT: 0px;")
txtstream.WriteLine ("    PADDING-LEFT: 0px;")
txtstream.WriteLine ("    PADDING-BOTTOM: 0px;")
txtstream.WriteLine ("    MARGIN: 0px;")
txtstream.WriteLine ("    COLOR: #333;")
txtstream.WriteLine ("    PADDING-TOP: 0px;")
txtstream.WriteLine ("    FONT-FAMILY: verdana, arial, helvetica, sans-serif;")
txtstream.WriteLine ("}")
txtstream.WriteLine ("table")
txtstream.WriteLine ("{")
txtstream.WriteLine ("    BORDER-RIGHT: #999999 1px solid;")
txtstream.WriteLine ("    PADDING-RIGHT: 1px;")
txtstream.WriteLine ("    PADDING-LEFT: 1px;")
txtstream.WriteLine ("    PADDING-BOTTOM: 1px;")
txtstream.WriteLine ("    LINE-HEIGHT: 8px;")
txtstream.WriteLine ("    PADDING-TOP: 1px;")
txtstream.WriteLine ("    BORDER-BOTTOM: #999 1px solid;")
txtstream.WriteLine ("    BACKGROUND-COLOR: #eeeeee;")
txtstream.WriteLine                                              ("
filter:progid:DXImageTransform.Microsoft.Shadow(color='silver',     Direction=135,
Strength=16)")
txtstream.WriteLine ("}")
txtstream.WriteLine ("th")
txtstream.WriteLine ("{")
txtstream.WriteLine ("    BORDER-RIGHT: #999999 3px solid;")
txtstream.WriteLine ("    PADDING-RIGHT: 6px;")
txtstream.WriteLine (",   PADDING-LEFT: 6px;")
txtstream.WriteLine ("    FONT-WEIGHT: Bold;")
txtstream.WriteLine ("    FONT-SIZE: 14px;")
```

```
txtstream.WriteLine ("    PADDING-BOTTOM: 6px;")
txtstream.WriteLine ("    COLOR: darkred;")
txtstream.WriteLine ("    LINE-HEIGHT: 14px;")
txtstream.WriteLine ("    PADDING-TOP: 6px;")
txtstream.WriteLine ("    BORDER-BOTTOM: #999 1px solid;")
txtstream.WriteLine ("    BACKGROUND-COLOR: #eeeeee;")
txtstream.WriteLine ("    FONT-FAMILY: font-family: Cambria, serif;")
txtstream.WriteLine ("    FONT-SIZE: 12px;")
txtstream.WriteLine ("    text-align: left;")
txtstream.WriteLine ("    white-Space: nowrap;")
txtstream.WriteLine ("}")
txtstream.WriteLine (".th")
txtstream.WriteLine ("{")
txtstream.WriteLine ("    BORDER-RIGHT: #999999 2px solid;")
txtstream.WriteLine ("    PADDING-RIGHT: 6px;")
txtstream.WriteLine ("    PADDING-LEFT: 6px;")
txtstream.WriteLine ("    FONT-WEIGHT: Bold;")
txtstream.WriteLine ("    PADDING-BOTTOM: 6px;")
txtstream.WriteLine ("    COLOR: black;")
txtstream.WriteLine ("    PADDING-TOP: 6px;")
txtstream.WriteLine ("    BORDER-BOTTOM: #999 2px solid;")
txtstream.WriteLine ("    BACKGROUND-COLOR: #eeeeee;")
txtstream.WriteLine ("    FONT-FAMILY: font-family: Cambria, serif;")
txtstream.WriteLine ("    FONT-SIZE: 10px;")
txtstream.WriteLine ("    text-align: right;")
txtstream.WriteLine ("    white-Space: nowrap;")
txtstream.WriteLine ("}")
txtstream.WriteLine ("td")
txtstream.WriteLine ("{")
txtstream.WriteLine ("    BORDER-RIGHT: #999999 3px solid;")
txtstream.WriteLine ("    PADDING-RIGHT: 6px;")
txtstream.WriteLine ("    PADDING-LEFT: 6px;")
txtstream.WriteLine ("    FONT-WEIGHT: Normal;")
```

```
txtstream.WriteLine ("    PADDING-BOTTOM: 6px;")
txtstream.WriteLine ("    COLOR: navy;")
txtstream.WriteLine ("    LINE-HEIGHT: 14px;")
txtstream.WriteLine ("    PADDING-TOP: 6px;")
txtstream.WriteLine ("    BORDER-BOTTOM: #999 1px solid;")
txtstream.WriteLine ("    BACKGROUND-COLOR: #eeeeee;")
txtstream.WriteLine ("    FONT-FAMILY: font-family: Cambria, serif;")
txtstream.WriteLine ("    FONT-SIZE: 12px;")
txtstream.WriteLine ("    text-align: left;")
txtstream.WriteLine ("    white-Space: nowrap;")
txtstream.WriteLine ("}")
txtstream.WriteLine ("div")
txtstream.WriteLine ("{")
txtstream.WriteLine ("    BORDER-RIGHT: #999999 3px solid;")
txtstream.WriteLine ("    PADDING-RIGHT: 6px;")
txtstream.WriteLine ("    PADDING-LEFT: 6px;")
txtstream.WriteLine ("    FONT-WEIGHT: Normal;")
txtstream.WriteLine ("    PADDING-BOTTOM: 6px;")
txtstream.WriteLine ("    COLOR: white;")
txtstream.WriteLine ("    PADDING-TOP: 6px;")
txtstream.WriteLine ("    BORDER-BOTTOM: #999 1px solid;")
txtstream.WriteLine ("    BACKGROUND-COLOR: navy;")
txtstream.WriteLine ("    FONT-FAMILY: font-family: Cambria, serif;")
txtstream.WriteLine ("    FONT-SIZE: 10px;")
txtstream.WriteLine ("    text-align: left;")
txtstream.WriteLine ("    white-Space: nowrap;")
txtstream.WriteLine ("}")
txtstream.WriteLine ("span")
txtstream.WriteLine ("{")
txtstream.WriteLine ("    BORDER-RIGHT: #999999 3px solid;")
txtstream.WriteLine ("    PADDING-RIGHT: 3px;")
txtstream.WriteLine ("    PADDING-LEFT: 3px;")
txtstream.WriteLine ("    FONT-WEIGHT: Normal;")
```

```
txtstream.WriteLine ("    PADDING-BOTTOM: 3px;")
txtstream.WriteLine ("    COLOR: white;")
txtstream.WriteLine ("    PADDING-TOP: 3px;")
txtstream.WriteLine ("    BORDER-BOTTOM: #999 1px solid;")
txtstream.WriteLine ("    BACKGROUND-COLOR: navy;")
txtstream.WriteLine ("    FONT-FAMILY: font-family: Cambria, serif;")
txtstream.WriteLine ("    FONT-SIZE: 10px;")
txtstream.WriteLine ("    text-align: left;")
txtstream.WriteLine ("    white-Space: nowrap;")
txtstream.WriteLine ("    display: inline-block;")
txtstream.WriteLine ("    width: 100%;")
txtstream.WriteLine ("}")
txtstream.WriteLine ("textarea")
txtstream.WriteLine ("{")
txtstream.WriteLine ("    BORDER-RIGHT: #999999 3px solid;")
txtstream.WriteLine ("    PADDING-RIGHT: 3px;")
txtstream.WriteLine ("    PADDING-LEFT: 3px;")
txtstream.WriteLine ("    FONT-WEIGHT: Normal;")
txtstream.WriteLine ("    PADDING-BOTTOM: 3px;")
txtstream.WriteLine ("    COLOR: white;")
txtstream.WriteLine ("    PADDING-TOP: 3px;")
txtstream.WriteLine ("    BORDER-BOTTOM: #999 1px solid;")
txtstream.WriteLine ("    BACKGROUND-COLOR: navy;")
txtstream.WriteLine ("    FONT-FAMILY: font-family: Cambria, serif;")
txtstream.WriteLine ("    FONT-SIZE: 10px;")
txtstream.WriteLine ("    text-align: left;")
txtstream.WriteLine ("    white-Space: nowrap;")
txtstream.WriteLine ("    width: 100%;")
txtstream.WriteLine ("}")
txtstream.WriteLine ("select")
txtstream.WriteLine ("{")
txtstream.WriteLine ("    BORDER-RIGHT: #999999 3px solid;")
txtstream.WriteLine ("    PADDING-RIGHT: 6px;")
```

```
txtstream.WriteLine ("    PADDING-LEFT: 6px;")
txtstream.WriteLine ("    FONT-WEIGHT: Normal;")
txtstream.WriteLine ("    PADDING-BOTTOM: 6px;")
txtstream.WriteLine ("    COLOR: white;")
txtstream.WriteLine ("    PADDING-TOP: 6px;")
txtstream.WriteLine ("    BORDER-BOTTOM: #999 1px solid;")
txtstream.WriteLine ("    BACKGROUND-COLOR: navy;")
txtstream.WriteLine ("    FONT-FAMILY: font-family: Cambria, serif;")
txtstream.WriteLine ("    FONT-SIZE: 10px;")
txtstream.WriteLine ("    text-align: left;")
txtstream.WriteLine ("    white-Space: nowrap;")
txtstream.WriteLine ("    width: 100%;")
txtstream.WriteLine ("}")
txtstream.WriteLine ("input")
txtstream.WriteLine ("{")
txtstream.WriteLine ("    BORDER-RIGHT: #999999 3px solid;")
txtstream.WriteLine ("    PADDING-RIGHT: 3px;")
txtstream.WriteLine ("    PADDING-LEFT: 3px;")
txtstream.WriteLine ("    FONT-WEIGHT: Bold;")
txtstream.WriteLine ("    PADDING-BOTTOM: 3px;")
txtstream.WriteLine ("    COLOR: white;")
txtstream.WriteLine ("    PADDING-TOP: 3px;")
txtstream.WriteLine ("    BORDER-BOTTOM: #999 1px solid;")
txtstream.WriteLine ("    BACKGROUND-COLOR: navy;")
txtstream.WriteLine ("    FONT-FAMILY: font-family: Cambria, serif;")
txtstream.WriteLine ("    FONT-SIZE: 12px;")
txtstream.WriteLine ("    text-align: left;")
txtstream.WriteLine ("    display: table-cell;")
txtstream.WriteLine ("    white-Space: nowrap;")
txtstream.WriteLine ("    width: 100%;")
txtstream.WriteLine ("}")
txtstream.WriteLine ("h1 {")
txtstream.WriteLine ("color: antiquewhite;")
```

```
txtstream.WriteLine ("text-shadow: 1px 1px 1px black;")
txtstream.WriteLine ("padding: 3px;")
txtstream.WriteLine ("text-align: center;")
txtstream.WriteLine ("box-shadow: inset 2px 2px 5px rgba(0,0,0,0.5), inset -2px -
2px 5px rgba(255,255,255,0.5);")
txtstream.WriteLine ("}")
txtstream.WriteLine ("</style>")


txtstream.WriteLine ("<title>Win32_Process</title>")
txtstream.WriteLine ("</head>")
txtstream.WriteLine ("<body>")
txtstream.WriteLine ("<table Border='1' cellpadding='1' cellspacing='1'>")
Set obj = objs.ItemIndex(0)
txtstream.WriteLine ("<tr>")
For Each prop In obj.Properties_
   txtstream.WriteLine ("<th>" & prop.Name & "</th>")
Next
txtstream.WriteLine ("</tr>")
For Each obj In objs
   txtstream.WriteLine ("<tr>")
   For Each prop In obj.Properties_
     txtstream.WriteLine     ("<td><input     type=""text""     value="""     &
GetValue(prop.Name, obj) & """></input></td>")
   Next
   txtstream.WriteLine ("</tr>")
Next
txtstream.WriteLine ("</table>")
txtstream.WriteLine ("</body>")
txtstream.WriteLine ("</html>")
txtstream.Close


End Sub
```

```
Function GetValue(ByVal Name, ByVal obj)

  Dim tempstr, pos, pName
  pName = Name
  tempstr = obj.GetObjectText_
  Name = Name + " = "
  pos = InStr(tempstr, Name)
  If pos Then

    pos = pos + Len(Name)
    tempstr = Mid(tempstr, pos, Len(tempstr))
    pos = InStr(tempstr, ";")
    tempstr = Mid(tempstr, 1, pos - 1)
    tempstr = Replace(tempstr, Chr(34), "")
    tempstr = Replace(tempstr, "{", "")
    tempstr = Replace(tempstr, "}", "")
    tempstr = Trim(tempstr)

    If obj.Properties_(pName).CIMType = 101 Then

      tempstr = Mid(tempstr, 5, 2) + "/" + _
          Mid(tempstr, 7, 2) + "/" + _
          Mid(tempstr, 1, 4) + " " + _
          Mid(tempstr, 9, 2) + ":" + _
          Mid(tempstr, 11, 2) + ":" + _
          Mid(tempstr, 13, 2)

  End If

  GetValue = tempstr
```

```
      Else

        GetValue = ""

      End If

End Function
```

Any of the routines below can be put into the Write_The_Output Sub routine. But one at a time, please.

Getting Started, Again
The Wbemscripting Primer

'm not going to waste time here, we have a lot to cover and I don't want to bore you with my ramblings.

The first thing you need to know about WbemScripting is why it was called Wbemscripting in the first place. The WBem part stands for Web Based Enterprise Management. The problem with it was – and still is – the concept was based on a Microsoft business model that says something over 7 years should be retired.

Well, if you go by my own awareness of the product, it should have been retired three times by now and it is still going strong and is growing in strength and power.

Bottom line, it is a beast!

But one you can handle because it is all based on Windows Management Instrumentation (WMI).

These are all optional and there is a rule which states when you are running this on the local machine you do not use UserName or Password.

Anyway, most of the examples you see on the web go like this:

```
Set locator = CreateObject("WbemScripting.SWbemLocator")
Set svc = locator.ConnectServer(".", "root\cimv2")
```

And that works perfectly fine, but if you really want the full power of the call:

Set locator = CreateObject("WbemScripting.SWbemLocator")

Set svc = locator.ConnectServer(".", "root\cimv2", "", "", "MS_409", "", 0 , Nothing)

And let's continue with this:

svc.Security_.AuthenticationLevel = 6 'PacketPrivacy

svc.Security_.ImpersonationLevel = 3 'Impersonate

svc.Security_.Privileges.Add()

svc.Security_.Privileges.Remove()

Past this point, the world of WMI gets much more complex, very quickly.

HOW WOULD YOU LIKE YOUR WMI?

Async or sync

Now, we're ready to go into interfaces that will help make this work to get the job done.

And you can use them in both Sync and Async mode.
Interface:

Get:

    Sync:

        Set objs = svc.Get("Win32_Process" &H2000)

    Async:

        Set mysink = CreateObject("WbemScripting.SWbemSink")
        Call svc.GetAsync(mysink, "Win32_Process", &H2000)

The primary purpose of this call is to find out if someone wrote a lengthy description on what the purpose of the properties are and what the values those properties mean. My experience with WMI tells me that most of the documented classes fall under the root\cimv2 namespace.

InstancesOf

Sync:
```
Set Objs = svc.InstancesOf("Win32_Process")
```

Async:
```
Set mysink = CreateObject("WbemScripting.SWbemSink")
Call svc.InstancesOfAsync(mysink, "Win32_Process")
```

The primary purpose of this call is to just get the information you want from the class without having to deal with an SQL or WQL query. It is the simplest to use and the workhorse of WbemScripting when you just want to glean the information from the class.

ExecNotificationQuery:

```
strQuery= "Select * From ___InstanceCreationEvent " +_
      "WITHIN 1 where TargetInstance ISA 'Win32_Process'")

strQuery= "Select * From ___InstanceDeletionEvent " +_
      "WITHIN 1 where TargetInstance ISA 'Win32_Process'")

strQuery= "Select * From ___InstanceModificationEvent " +_
      "WITHIN 1 where TargetInstance ISA 'Win32_Process'")

strQuery= "Select * From ___InstanceOperationEvent " +_
      "WITHIN 1 where TargetInstance ISA 'Win32_Process'")
```

Sync:

Set es = ExecNotificationQuery(strQuery)

Async:

Set mysink = CreateObject("WbemScripting.SWbemSink")
Call svc.ExecNotificationQueryAsync(mysink, strQuery)

This is the heart of many calls made through WMI to determine if an event has occurred that you want to know about. The ___InstanceOperationEvent is combination of all three. You just filter through the events to know if it is the one you are looking for and what type of event it is.

ExecQuery:

Sync:

Set ob = svc.ExecQuery("Select * From Win32_Process")

Async:

Set mysink = CreateObject("WbemScripting.SWbemSink")
Call svc.ExecQueryAsync(mysink, "Select * From Win32_Process")

This call allows you to filter through all or some of the properties that could be returned and query for a specific value.

A Full Async Example

Belov, is a full async example.

```
Option Explicit

Dim sink
Dim ns
Dim Classname
Dim v
Dim w

Private Sub sink_OnObjectReady(ByVal objWbemObject, ByVal objWbemAsyncContext)

    For Each prop in objWbemObject.Properties_
        v = v + prop.Name & " " & GetValue(prop.Name, objWbemObject) & vbCrLf
    Next
    MsgBox (v)

End Sub
```

```
Private Sub sink_OnCompleted(ByVal iHResult, ByVal objWbemErrorObject,
ByVal objWbemAsyncContext)
      w = 1

End Sub

w = 0
ns = "root\Cimv2"
Classname = "Win32_Process"
Set locator = CreateObject("WbemScripting.SWbemLocator")
Set svc = locator.ConnectServer(".", ns)
svc.Security_.AuthenticationLevel = 6
svc.Security_.ImpersonationLevel = 3

Set sink = WScript.CreateObject("WBemScripting.SWbemSink", "SINK_")
Call svc.ExecQueryAsync(sink, "Select * From " & Classname)

Do While w = 0
  WScript.Sleep(500)
Loop


Function GetValue(ByVal Name, ByVal obj)

  Dim tempstr, pos, pName
  pName = Name
  tempstr = obj.GetObjectText_
  Name = Name + " = "
  pos = InStr(tempstr, Name)
  If pos Then

    pos = pos + Len(Name)
    tempstr = Mid(tempstr, pos, Len(tempstr))
```

```
    pos = InStr(tempstr, ";")
    tempstr = Mid(tempstr, 1, pos - 1)
    tempstr = Replace(tempstr, Chr(34), "")
    tempstr = Replace(tempstr, "{", "")
    tempstr = Replace(tempstr, "}", "")
    tempstr = Trim(tempstr)

    If obj.Properties_(pName).CIMType = 101 Then

       tempstr = Mid(tempstr, 5, 2) + "/" + _
             Mid(tempstr, 7, 2) + "/" + _
             Mid(tempstr, 1, 4) + " " + _
             Mid(tempstr, 9, 2) + ":" + _
             Mid(tempstr, 11, 2) + ":" + _
             Mid(tempstr, 13, 2)

    End If

    GetValue = tempstr

  Else

    GetValue = ""

  End If

End Function
```

A Full Sync Example

B ELOW, IS A FULL SYNC EXAMPLE.

```
On Error Resume Next
Dim ns
Dim Classname
Dim v
ns = "root\Cimv2"
Classname = "Win32_Process"

Set locator = CreateObject("WbemScripting.SWbemLocator")
Set svc = locator.ConnectServer(".",  "root\cimV2")
svc.Security_.AuthenticationLevel=6")
svc.Security_.ImpersonationLevel=3")
Set objs = svc.InstancesOf("Win32_Process")

For each obj in objs
   For each prop in obj.Properties_
     v=v + prop.Name & " " & getValue(prop.Name, obj) & vbcrlf
   Next
```

```vbscript
Next

WScript.Echo(v)

Function GetValue(ByVal Name, ByVal obj)

  Dim tempstr, pos, pName
  pName = Name
  tempstr = obj.GetObjectText_
  Name = Name + " = "
  pos = InStr(tempstr, Name)
  If pos Then

    pos = pos + Len(Name)
    tempstr = Mid(tempstr, pos, Len(tempstr))
    pos = InStr(tempstr, ";")
    tempstr = Mid(tempstr, 1, pos - 1)
    tempstr = Replace(tempstr, Chr(34), "")
    tempstr = Replace(tempstr, "{", "")
    tempstr = Replace(tempstr, "}", "")
    tempstr = Trim(tempstr)
    If obj.Properties_(pName).CIMType = 101 Then

      tempstr = Mid(tempstr, 5, 2) + "/" + _
            Mid(tempstr, 7, 2) + "/" + _
            Mid(tempstr, 1, 4) + " " + _
            Mid(tempstr, 9, 2) + ":" + _
            Mid(tempstr, 11, 2) + ":" + _
            Mid(tempstr, 11, 2) + ":" + _
            Mid(tempstr, 13, 2)

    End If
```

```
            GetValue = tempstr

        Else

            GetValue = ""

        End If

    End Function
```

The Many ways to use your WMI skills and impress people

The following is list of the what we're going to be using with WMI:

ASP

ASPX

Attribute XML

Delimited Files

Element XML

Element XML For XSL

Excel

HTA

HTML

Schema XML

XSL

I need to do this before someone complains.

Up to here, the various languages I'm going to cover will have the same chapters. But past here, the code is specifically for each language. All will have the same code examples but written in the language specified in the title.

Working with ASP
The concept of programs writing programs

NEED TO SHARE SOMETHING IMPOTANT WITH YOU THAT I HAVE SEEN ASKED BY PROS OVER AND OVER AGAIN. THE FACT THAT THEY ARE ASKING IT SHOWS JUST HOW UNAWARE THEY ARE OF THIS IMPORTANT FACT. Anything you write inside a textstream is considered by the compiler to be a string and not code.

So, if I type:

For VBScript, VB, VBS, VB.Net, Python, Ruby:

```
txtstream.WriteLine("Response.Write(""<tr>"" & vbcrlf) ")
```

For Javascript, JScript:

```
txtstream.WriteLine("Response.Write(""<tr>"" & vbcrlf) ");
```

For Kixtart:

```
$txtstream.WriteLine("Response.Write(""<tr>"" & vbcrlf) ")
```

For C#:

```
txtstream.WriteLine("Response.Write(\"<tr>\" & vbcrlf) ");
```

For C++:

```
txtstream->WriteLine("Response.Write(\"<tr>\" & vbcrlf) ");
```

For Perlscript:

```
$txtstream->WriteLine("Response.Write(""<tr>"" & vbcrlf) ");
```

For Rexx:

```
txtstream~WriteLine("Response.Write(""<tr>"" & vbcrlf) ")
```

For Borland C Builder:

txtstream.OLEFunction("WriteLine", OleVariant("Response.Write(""<tr>""" & vbcrlf) ");

For Borland Delphi:

txtstream.WriteLine('Response.Write("<tr> " & vbcrlf) ');

Aside from conforming to the compiler's expectations for single and double quotes, see any difference in the Response.Write("<tr>" & vbcrlf). It's because that part of the code is written to run as VBScript.

That also means any of the 14 languages listed could also create any of the other 14 languages. Hence, Programs that write programs. Below, is the code for ASP. The getValue function is in Appendix B.

```
Set ws = CreateObject("WScript.Shell")
Set fso = CreateObject("Scripting.FileSystemObject")
Set txtstream = fso.OpenTextFile(ws.CurrentDirectory + "\Win32_Process.asp", 2, true, -2)
```

For Single Line Horizontal

```
txtstream.WriteLine("<html>")
txtstream.WriteLine("<head>")
txtstream.WriteLine("<style type='text/css'>")
txtstream.WriteLine("th")
txtstream.WriteLine("{")
txtstream.WriteLine("   COLOR: darkred;")
txtstream.WriteLine("   BACKGROUND-COLOR: white;")
txtstream.WriteLine("   FONT-FAMILY:font-family: Cambria, serif;")
txtstream.WriteLine("   FONT-SIZE: 12px;")
txtstream.WriteLine("   text-align: left;")
txtstream.WriteLine("   white-Space: nowrap;")
txtstream.WriteLine("}")
txtstream.WriteLine("td")
```

```
txtstream.WriteLine("{")
txtstream.WriteLine("    COLOR: navy;")
txtstream.WriteLine("    BACKGROUND-COLOR: white;")
txtstream.WriteLine("    FONT-FAMILY: font-family: Cambria, serif;")
txtstream.WriteLine("    FONT-SIZE: 12px;")
txtstream.WriteLine("    text-align: left;")
txtstream.WriteLine("    white-Space: nowrap;")
txtstream.WriteLine("}")
txtstream.WriteLine("</style>")
txtstream.WriteLine("<title>Win32_Process</title>")
txtstream.WriteLine("</head>")
txtstream.WriteLine("<body>")
```

Use this if you want to create a border around your table:

```
txtstream.WriteLine("<table Border='1' cellpadding='1' cellspacing='1'>")
```

Use this if you don't want to create a border around your table:

```
txtstream.WriteLine("<table Border='0' cellpadding='1' cellspacing='1'>")
```

```
txtstream.WriteLine("<%")
Set obj = objs.ItemIndex(0)
txtstream.WriteLine("Response.Write(""<tr>"" & vbcrlf)")
for each prop in obj.Properties_
    txtstream.WriteLine("Response.Write(""<th>" & prop.Name & "</th>"" & vbcrlf)")
next
txtstream.WriteLine("Response.Write(""</tr>"" & vbcrlf)")
txtstream.WriteLine("Response.Write(""<tr>"" & vbcrlf)")

for each prop in obj.Properties_
    txtstream.WriteLine("Response.Write(""<td>" & GetValue(prop.Name, obj) & "</td>"" & vbcrlf)")
next
```

```
txtstream.WriteLine("Response.Write(""</tr>"" & vbcrlf)")
txtstream.WriteLine("%>")
txtstream.WriteLine("</table>")
txtstream.WriteLine("</body>")
txtstream.WriteLine("</html>")
txtstream.close
```

For Multi Line Horizontal

```
txtstream.WriteLine("<html>")
txtstream.WriteLine("<head>")
txtstream.WriteLine("<style type='text/css'>")
txtstream.WriteLine("th")
txtstream.WriteLine("{")
txtstream.WriteLine("    COLOR: darkred;")
txtstream.WriteLine("    BACKGROUND-COLOR: white;")
txtstream.WriteLine("    FONT-FAMILY:font-family: Cambria, serif;")
txtstream.WriteLine("    FONT-SIZE: 12px;")
txtstream.WriteLine("    text-align: left;")
txtstream.WriteLine("    white-Space: nowrap;")
txtstream.WriteLine("}")
txtstream.WriteLine("td")
txtstream.WriteLine("{")
txtstream.WriteLine("    COLOR: navy;")
txtstream.WriteLine("    BACKGROUND-COLOR: white;")
txtstream.WriteLine("    FONT-FAMILY: font-family: Cambria, serif;")
txtstream.WriteLine("    FONT-SIZE: 12px;")
txtstream.WriteLine("    text-align: left;")
txtstream.WriteLine("    white-Space: nowrap;")
txtstream.WriteLine("}")
txtstream.WriteLine("</style>")
txtstream.WriteLine("<title>Win32_Process</title>")
```

```
txtstream.WriteLine("</head>")
txtstream.WriteLine("<body>")
```

Use this if you want to create a border around your table:
```
txtstream.WriteLine("<table Border='1' cellpadding='1' cellspacing='1'>")
```

Use this if you don't want to create a border around your table:
```
txtstream.WriteLine("<table Border='0' cellpadding='1' cellspacing='1'>")
```

```
txtstream.WriteLine("<%")
Set obj = objs.ItemIndex(0)
txtstream.WriteLine("Response.Write(""<tr>"" & vbcrlf)")
for each prop in obj.Properties_
    txtstream.WriteLine("Response.Write(""<th>" & prop.Name & "</th>"" & vbcrlf)")
next
txtstream.WriteLine("Response.Write(""</tr>"" & vbcrlf)")
for each obj in objs
    txtstream.WriteLine("Response.Write(""<tr>"" & vbcrlf)")
    for each prop in obj.Properties_
        txtstream.WriteLine("Response.Write(""<td>" & GetValue(prop.Name, obj) & "</td>"" & vbcrlf)")
    next
    txtstream.WriteLine("Response.Write(""</tr>"" & vbcrlf)")
Next
txtstream.WriteLine("%>")
txtstream.WriteLine("</table>")
txtstream.WriteLine("</body>")
txtstream.WriteLine("</html>")
txtstream.close
```

For Single Line Vertical

```
txtstream.WriteLine("<html>")
```

```
txtstream.WriteLine("<head>")
txtstream.WriteLine("<style type='text/css'>")
txtstream.WriteLine("th")
txtstream.WriteLine("{")
txtstream.WriteLine("   COLOR: darkred;")
txtstream.WriteLine("   BACKGROUND-COLOR: white;")
txtstream.WriteLine("   FONT-FAMILY:font-family: Cambria, serif;")
txtstream.WriteLine("   FONT-SIZE: 12px;")
txtstream.WriteLine("   text-align: left;")
txtstream.WriteLine("   white-Space: nowrap;")
txtstream.WriteLine("}")
txtstream.WriteLine("td")
txtstream.WriteLine("{")
txtstream.WriteLine("   COLOR: navy;")
txtstream.WriteLine("   BACKGROUND-COLOR: white;")
txtstream.WriteLine("   FONT-FAMILY: font-family: Cambria, serif;")
txtstream.WriteLine("   FONT-SIZE: 12px;")
txtstream.WriteLine("   text-align: left;")
txtstream.WriteLine("   white-Space: nowrap;")
txtstream.WriteLine("}")
txtstream.WriteLine("</style>")
txtstream.WriteLine("<title>Win32_Process</title>")
txtstream.WriteLine("</head>")
txtstream.WriteLine("<body>")
```

Use this if you want to create a border around your table:
```
txtstream.WriteLine("<table Border='1' cellpadding='1' cellspacing='1'>")
```

Use this if you don't want to create a border around your table:
```
txtstream.WriteLine("<table Border='0' cellpadding='1' cellspacing='1'>")
```

```
txtstream.WriteLine("<%")
Set obj = objs.ItemIndex(0)
```

```
    for each prop in obj.Properties_
        txtstream.WriteLine("Response.Write(""<tr><th>"        &        prop.Name        &
"</th><td>" & GetValue(prop.Name, obj) & "</td></tr>""" & vbcrlf)")
    next
    txtstream.WriteLine("%>")
    txtstream.WriteLine("</table>")
    txtstream.WriteLine("</body>")
    txtstream.WriteLine("</html>")
    txtstream.close
```

For Multi Line Vertical

```
    txtstream.WriteLine("<html>")
    txtstream.WriteLine("<head>")
    txtstream.WriteLine("<style type='text/css'>")
    txtstream.WriteLine("th")
    txtstream.WriteLine("{")
    txtstream.WriteLine("    COLOR: darkred;")
    txtstream.WriteLine("    BACKGROUND-COLOR: white;")
    txtstream.WriteLine("    FONT-FAMILY:font-family: Cambria, serif;")
    txtstream.WriteLine("    FONT-SIZE: 12px;")
    txtstream.WriteLine("    text-align: left;")
    txtstream.WriteLine("    white-Space: nowrap;")
    txtstream.WriteLine("}")
    txtstream.WriteLine("td")
    txtstream.WriteLine("{")
    txtstream.WriteLine("    COLOR: navy;")
    txtstream.WriteLine("    BACKGROUND-COLOR: white;")
    txtstream.WriteLine("    FONT-FAMILY: font-family: Cambria, serif;")
    txtstream.WriteLine("    FONT-SIZE: 12px;")
    txtstream.WriteLine("    text-align: left;")
    txtstream.WriteLine("    white-Space: nowrap;")
    txtstream.WriteLine("}")
```

```
txtstream.WriteLine("</style>")
txtstream.WriteLine("<title>Win32_Process</title>")
txtstream.WriteLine("</head>")
txtstream.WriteLine("<body>")
```

Use this if you want to create a border around your table:
```
txtstream.WriteLine("<table Border='1' cellpadding='1' cellspacing='1'>")
```

Use this if you don't want to create a border around your table:
```
txtstream.WriteLine("<table Border='0' cellpadding='1' cellspacing='1'>")
txtstream.WriteLine("<%")
Set obj = objs.ItemIndex(0)
for each prop in obj.Properties_
    txtstream.WriteLine("Response.Write(""<tr><th>" & prop.Name & "</th>""" 
& vbcrlf)")
        for each obj in objs
            txtstream.WriteLine("Response.Write(""<td>"  &   GetValue(prop.Name, 
obj) & "</td>""" & vbcrlf)")
        next
        txtstream.WriteLine("Response.Write(""</tr>""" & vbcrlf)")
    Next
txtstream.WriteLine("%>")
txtstream.WriteLine("</table>")
txtstream.WriteLine("</body>")
txtstream.WriteLine("</html>")
txtstream.close
```

ASPX Code

Below, is the code for ASP. The getValue function is in Appendix B.

Set ws = CreateObject("WScript.Shell")

Set fso = CreateObject("Scripting.FileSystemObject")

Set txtstream = fso.OpenTextFile(ws.CurrentDirectory + "\Win32_Process.aspx", 2, true, -2)

For Single Line Horizontal

txtstream.WriteLine("<!DOCTYPE html PUBLIC ""-//W3C//DTD XHTML 1.0 Transitional//EN"" ""http://www.w3.org/TR/xhtml1/DTD/xhtml1-transitional.dtd"">")

txtstream.WriteLine("")

txtstream.WriteLine("<html xmlns="http://www.w3.org/1999/xhtml" >")

txtstream.WriteLine("<head>")

txtstream.WriteLine("<style type='text/css'>")

txtstream.WriteLine("th")

txtstream.WriteLine("{")

txtstream.WriteLine("   COLOR: darkred;")

txtstream.WriteLine("   BACKGROUND-COLOR: white;")

txtstream.WriteLine("   FONT-FAMILY:font-family: Cambria, serif;")

```
txtstream.WriteLine("    FONT-SIZE: 12px;")
txtstream.WriteLine("    text-align: left;")
txtstream.WriteLine("    white-Space: nowrap;")
txtstream.WriteLine("}")
txtstream.WriteLine("td")
txtstream.WriteLine("{")
txtstream.WriteLine("    COLOR: navy;")
txtstream.WriteLine("    BACKGROUND-COLOR: white;")
txtstream.WriteLine("    FONT-FAMILY: font-family: Cambria, serif;")
txtstream.WriteLine("    FONT-SIZE: 12px;")
txtstream.WriteLine("    text-align: left;")
txtstream.WriteLine("    white-Space: nowrap;")
txtstream.WriteLine("}")
txtstream.WriteLine("</style>")
txtstream.WriteLine("<title>Win32_Process</title>")
txtstream.WriteLine("</head>")
txtstream.WriteLine("<body>")
```

Use this if you want to create a border around your table:
```
txtstream.WriteLine("<table Border='1' cellpadding='1' cellspacing='1'>")
```

Use this if you don't want to create a border around your table:
```
txtstream.WriteLine("<table Border='0' cellpadding='1' cellspacing='1'>")
txtstream.WriteLine("<%")
Set obj = objs.ItemIndex(0)
txtstream.WriteLine("Response.Write(""<tr>"" & vbcrlf)")
for each prop in obj.Properties_
    txtstream.WriteLine("Response.Write(""<th>" & prop.Name & "</th>"" & vbcrlf)")
    next
txtstream.WriteLine("Response.Write(""</tr>"" & vbcrlf)")
txtstream.WriteLine("Response.Write(""<tr>"" & vbcrlf)")
for each prop in obj.Properties_
```

```
        txtstream.WriteLine("Response.Write(""<td>" & GetValue(prop.Name, obj)
& "</td>"" & vbcrlf)")
    next
    txtstream.WriteLine("Response.Write(""</tr>"" & vbcrlf)")
    txtstream.WriteLine("%>")
    txtstream.WriteLine("</table>")
    txtstream.WriteLine("</body>")
    txtstream.WriteLine("</html>")
    txtstream.close
```

For Multi Line Horizontal

```
    txtstream.WriteLine("<!DOCTYPE html PUBLIC ""-//W3C//DTD XHTML 1.0
Transitional//EN"" ""http://www.w3.org/TR/xhtml1/DTD/xhtml1-
transitional.dtd"">")
    txtstream.WriteLine("")
    txtstream.WriteLine("<html xmlns="http://www.w3.org/1999/xhtml"
>")
    txtstream.WriteLine("<head>")
    txtstream.WriteLine("<style type='text/css'>")
    txtstream.WriteLine("th")
    txtstream.WriteLine("{")
    txtstream.WriteLine("   COLOR: darkred;")
    txtstream.WriteLine("   BACKGROUND-COLOR: white;")
    txtstream.WriteLine("   FONT-FAMILY:font-family: Cambria, serif;")
    txtstream.WriteLine("   FONT-SIZE: 12px;")
    txtstream.WriteLine("   text-align: left;")
    txtstream.WriteLine("   white-Space: nowrap;")
    txtstream.WriteLine("}")
    txtstream.WriteLine("td")
    txtstream.WriteLine("{")
    txtstream.WriteLine("   COLOR: navy;")
    txtstream.WriteLine("   BACKGROUND-COLOR: white;")
    txtstream.WriteLine("   FONT-FAMILY: font-family: Cambria, serif;")
```

```
txtstream.WriteLine("   FONT-SIZE: 12px;")
txtstream.WriteLine("   text-align: left;")
txtstream.WriteLine("   white-Space: nowrap;")
txtstream.WriteLine("}")
txtstream.WriteLine("</style>")
txtstream.WriteLine("<title>Win32_Process</title>")
txtstream.WriteLine("</head>")
txtstream.WriteLine("<body>")
```

Use this if you want to create a border around your table:

```
txtstream.WriteLine("<table Border='1' cellpadding='1' cellspacing='1'>")
```

Use this if you don't want to create a border around your table:

```
txtstream.WriteLine("<table Border='0' cellpadding='1' cellspacing='1'>")
```

```
txtstream.WriteLine("<%")
Set obj = objs.ItemIndex(0)
txtstream.WriteLine("Response.Write(""<tr>"" & vbcrlf)")
for each prop in obj.Properties_
    txtstream.WriteLine("Response.Write(""<th>" & prop.Name & "</th>"" & vbcrlf)")
    next
txtstream.WriteLine("Response.Write(""</tr>"" & vbcrlf)")
for each obj in objs
    txtstream.WriteLine("Response.Write(""<tr>"" & vbcrlf)")
    for each prop in obj.Properties_
        txtstream.WriteLine("Response.Write(""<td>" & GetValue(prop.Name, obj) & "</td>"" & vbcrlf)")
    next
    txtstream.WriteLine("Response.Write(""</tr>"" & vbcrlf)")
Next
txtstream.WriteLine("%>")
txtstream.WriteLine("</table>")
```

```
txtstream.WriteLine("</body>")
txtstream.WriteLine("</html>")
txtstream.close
```

For Single Line Vertical

```
txtstream.WriteLine("<!DOCTYPE html PUBLIC ""-//W3C//DTD XHTML 1.0
Transitional//EN"" ""http://www.w3.org/TR/xhtml1/DTD/xhtml1-
transitional.dtd"">")
txtstream.WriteLine("")
txtstream.WriteLine("<html xmlns="http://www.w3.org/1999/xhtml"
>")
txtstream.WriteLine("<head>")
txtstream.WriteLine("<style type='text/css'>")
txtstream.WriteLine("th")
txtstream.WriteLine("{")
txtstream.WriteLine("   COLOR: darkred;")
txtstream.WriteLine("   BACKGROUND-COLOR: white;")
txtstream.WriteLine("   FONT-FAMILY:font-family: Cambria, serif;")
txtstream.WriteLine("   FONT-SIZE: 12px;")
txtstream.WriteLine("   text-align: left;")
txtstream.WriteLine("   white-Space: nowrap;")
txtstream.WriteLine("}")
txtstream.WriteLine("td")
txtstream.WriteLine("{")
txtstream.WriteLine("   COLOR: navy;")
txtstream.WriteLine("   BACKGROUND-COLOR: white;")
txtstream.WriteLine("   FONT-FAMILY: font-family: Cambria, serif;")
txtstream.WriteLine("   FONT-SIZE: 12px;")
txtstream.WriteLine("   text-align: left;")
txtstream.WriteLine("   white-Space: nowrap;")
txtstream.WriteLine("}")
txtstream.WriteLine("</style>")
txtstream.WriteLine("<title>Win32_Process</title>")
txtstream.WriteLine("</head>")
```

```
txtstream.WriteLine("<body>")
```

Use this if you want to create a border around your table:
```
txtstream.WriteLine("<table Border='1' cellpadding='1' cellspacing='1'>")
```

Use this if you don't want to create a border around your table:
```
txtstream.WriteLine("<table Border='0' cellpadding='1' cellspacing='1'>")
```

```
txtstream.WriteLine("<%")
Set obj = objs.ItemIndex(0)
for each prop in obj.Properties_
    txtstream.WriteLine("Response.Write(""<tr><th>"        &        prop.Name        &
"</th><td>" & GetValue(prop.Name, obj) & "</td></tr>""" & vbcrlf)")
next
txtstream.WriteLine("%>")
txtstream.WriteLine("</table>")
txtstream.WriteLine("</body>")
txtstream.WriteLine("</html>")
txtstream.close
```

For Multi Line Vertical

```
txtstream.WriteLine("<!DOCTYPE html PUBLIC ""-//W3C//DTD XHTML 1.0
Transitional//EN"" ""http://www.w3.org/TR/xhtml1/DTD/xhtml1-
transitional.dtd"">")
txtstream.WriteLine("")
txtstream.WriteLine("<html xmlns="http://www.w3.org/1999/xhtml"
>")
txtstream.WriteLine("<head>")
txtstream.WriteLine("<style type='text/css'>")
txtstream.WriteLine("th")
txtstream.WriteLine("{")
txtstream.WriteLine("   COLOR: darkred;")
txtstream.WriteLine("   BACKGROUND-COLOR: white;")
```

```
txtstream.WriteLine("   FONT-FAMILY:font-family: Cambria, serif;")
txtstream.WriteLine("   FONT-SIZE: 12px;")
txtstream.WriteLine("   text-align: left;")
txtstream.WriteLine("   white-Space: nowrap;")
txtstream.WriteLine("}")
txtstream.WriteLine("td")
txtstream.WriteLine("{")
txtstream.WriteLine("   COLOR: navy;")
txtstream.WriteLine("   BACKGROUND-COLOR: white;")
txtstream.WriteLine("   FONT-FAMILY: font-family: Cambria, serif;")
txtstream.WriteLine("   FONT-SIZE: 12px;")
txtstream.WriteLine("   text-align: left;")
txtstream.WriteLine("   white-Space: nowrap;")
txtstream.WriteLine("}")
txtstream.WriteLine("</style>")
txtstream.WriteLine("<title>Win32_Process</title>")
txtstream.WriteLine("</head>")
txtstream.WriteLine("<body>")
```

Use this if you want to create a border around your table:
```
txtstream.WriteLine("<table Border='1' cellpadding='1' cellspacing='1'>")
```

Use this if you don't want to create a border around your table:
```
txtstream.WriteLine("<table Border='0' cellpadding='1' cellspacing='1'>")
```

```
txtstream.WriteLine("<%")
Set obj = objs.ItemIndex(0)
for each prop in obj.Properties_
    txtstream.WriteLine("Response.Write(""<tr><th>" & prop.Name & "</th>""" 
& vbcrlf)")
        for each obj in objs
        txtstream.WriteLine("Response.Write(""<td>"   &   GetValue(prop.Name, 
obj) & "</td>""" & vbcrlf)")
```

```
        next
        txtstream.WriteLine("Response.Write(""</tr>"" & vbcrlf)")
Next
txtstream.WriteLine("%>")
txtstream.WriteLine("</table>")
txtstream.WriteLine("</body>")
txtstream.WriteLine("</html>")
txtstream.close
```

HTA Code

Below, is the code for HTA. The getValue function is in Appendix B.

```
Set ws = CreateObject("WScript.Shell")
Set fso = CreateObject("Scripting.FileSystemObject")
Set txtstream = fso.OpenTextFile(ws.CurrentDirectory + "\Win32_Process.hta",
2, true, -2)
```

For Single Line Horizontal

```
txtstream.WriteLine("<html>")
txtstream.WriteLine("<head>")
txtstream.WriteLine("<HTA:APPLICATION ")
txtstream.WriteLine("ID = ""Process"" ")
txtstream.WriteLine("APPLICATIONNAME = ""Process"" ")
txtstream.WriteLine("SCROLL = ""yes"" ")
txtstream.WriteLine("SINGLEINSTANCE = ""yes"" ")
txtstream.WriteLine("WINDOWSTATE = ""maximize"" >")
txtstream.WriteLine("<style type='text/css'>")
txtstream.WriteLine("th")
txtstream.WriteLine("{")
```

```
txtstream.WriteLine("    COLOR: darkred;")
txtstream.WriteLine("    BACKGROUND-COLOR: white;")
txtstream.WriteLine("    FONT-FAMILY:font-family: Cambria, serif;")
txtstream.WriteLine("    FONT-SIZE: 12px;")
txtstream.WriteLine("    text-align: left;")
txtstream.WriteLine("    white-Space: nowrap;")
txtstream.WriteLine("}")
txtstream.WriteLine("td")
txtstream.WriteLine("{")
txtstream.WriteLine("    COLOR: navy;")
txtstream.WriteLine("    BACKGROUND-COLOR: white;")
txtstream.WriteLine("    FONT-FAMILY: font-family: Cambria, serif;")
txtstream.WriteLine("    FONT-SIZE: 12px;")
txtstream.WriteLine("    text-align: left;")
txtstream.WriteLine("    white-Space: nowrap;")
txtstream.WriteLine("}")
txtstream.WriteLine("</style>")
txtstream.WriteLine("<title>Win32_Process</title>")
txtstream.WriteLine("</head>")
txtstream.WriteLine("<body>")
```

Use this if you want to create a border around your table:
```
txtstream.WriteLine("<table Border='1' cellpadding='1' cellspacing='1'>")
```

Use this if you don't want to create a border around your table:
```
txtstream.WriteLine("<table Border='0' cellpadding='1' cellspacing='1'>")
Set obj = objs.ItemIndex(0)
txtstream.WriteLine("<tr>")
for each prop in obj.Properties_
    txtstream.WriteLine("<th>" & prop.Name & "</th>")
next
txtstream.WriteLine("</tr>")
txtstream.WriteLine("<tr>")
```

```
for each prop in obj.Properties_
    txtstream.WriteLine("<td>" & GetValue(prop.Name, obj) & "</td>")
next
txtstream.WriteLine("</tr>")
txtstream.WriteLine("</table>")
txtstream.WriteLine("</body>")
txtstream.WriteLine("</html>")
txtstream.close
```

For Multi Line Horizontal

```
txtstream.WriteLine(html>")
txtstream.WriteLine("<head>")
txtstream.WriteLine("<HTA:APPLICATION ")
txtstream.WriteLine("ID = ""Process"" ")
txtstream.WriteLine("APPLICATIONNAME = ""Process"" ")
txtstream.WriteLine("SCROLL = ""yes"" ")
txtstream.WriteLine("SINGLEINSTANCE = ""yes"" ")
txtstream.WriteLine("WINDOWSTATE = ""maximize"" >")
txtstream.WriteLine("<style type='text/css'>")
txtstream.WriteLine("th")
txtstream.WriteLine("{")
txtstream.WriteLine("   COLOR: darkred;")
txtstream.WriteLine("   BACKGROUND-COLOR: white;")
txtstream.WriteLine("   FONT-FAMILY:font-family: Cambria, serif;")
txtstream.WriteLine("   FONT-SIZE: 12px;")
txtstream.WriteLine("   text-align: left;")
txtstream.WriteLine("   white-Space: nowrap;")
txtstream.WriteLine("}")
txtstream.WriteLine("td")
txtstream.WriteLine("{")
txtstream.WriteLine("   COLOR: navy;")
txtstream.WriteLine("   BACKGROUND-COLOR: white;")
```

```
txtstream.WriteLine("    FONT-FAMILY: font-family: Cambria, serif;")
txtstream.WriteLine("    FONT-SIZE: 12px;")
txtstream.WriteLine("    text-align: left;")
txtstream.WriteLine("    white-Space: nowrap;")
txtstream.WriteLine("}")
txtstream.WriteLine("</style>")
txtstream.WriteLine("<title>Win32_Process</title>")
txtstream.WriteLine("</head>")
txtstream.WriteLine("<body>")
```

Use this if you want to create a border around your table:
```
txtstream.WriteLine("<table Border='1' cellpadding='1' cellspacing='1'>")
```

Use this if you don't want to create a border around your table:
```
txtstream.WriteLine("<table Border='0' cellpadding='1' cellspacing='1'>")
```

```
Set obj = objs.ItemIndex(0)
txtstream.WriteLine("<tr>")
for each prop in obj.Properties_
   txtstream.WriteLine("<th>" & prop.Name & "</th>")
next
txtstream.WriteLine("</tr>")
for each obj in objs
   txtstream.WriteLine("<tr>")
   for each prop in obj.Properties_
      txtstream.WriteLine("<td>" & GetValue(prop.Name, obj) & "</td>")
   next
   txtstream.WriteLine("</tr>")
Next
txtstream.WriteLine("</table>")
txtstream.WriteLine("</body>")
txtstream.WriteLine("</html>")
txtstream.close
```

For Single Line Vertical

```
txtstream.WriteLine("<html>")
txtstream.WriteLine("<head>")
txtstream.WriteLine("<HTA:APPLICATION ")
txtstream.WriteLine("ID = ""Process"" ")
txtstream.WriteLine("APPLICATIONNAME = ""Process"" ")
txtstream.WriteLine("SCROLL = ""yes"" ")
txtstream.WriteLine("SINGLEINSTANCE = ""yes"" ")
txtstream.WriteLine("WINDOWSTATE = ""maximize"" >")
txtstream.WriteLine("<style type='text/css'>")
txtstream.WriteLine("th")
txtstream.WriteLine("{")
txtstream.WriteLine("   COLOR: darkred;")
txtstream.WriteLine("   BACKGROUND-COLOR: white;")
txtstream.WriteLine("   FONT-FAMILY:font-family: Cambria, serif;")
txtstream.WriteLine("   FONT-SIZE: 12px;")
txtstream.WriteLine("   text-align: left;")
txtstream.WriteLine("   white-Space: nowrap;")
txtstream.WriteLine("}")
txtstream.WriteLine("td")
txtstream.WriteLine("{")
txtstream.WriteLine("   COLOR: navy;")
txtstream.WriteLine("   BACKGROUND-COLOR: white;")
txtstream.WriteLine("   FONT-FAMILY: font-family: Cambria, serif;")
txtstream.WriteLine("   FONT-SIZE: 12px;")
txtstream.WriteLine("   text-align: left;")
txtstream.WriteLine("   white-Space: nowrap;")
txtstream.WriteLine("}")
txtstream.WriteLine("</style>")
txtstream.WriteLine("<title>Win32_Process</title>")
```

```
txtstream.WriteLine("</head>")
txtstream.WriteLine("<body>")
```

Use this if you want to create a border around your table:

```
txtstream.WriteLine("<table Border='1' cellpadding='1' cellspacing='1'>")
```

Use this if you don't want to create a border around your table:

```
txtstream.WriteLine("<table Border='0' cellpadding='1' cellspacing='1'>")
```

```
Set obj = objs.ItemIndex(0)
for each prop in obj.Properties_
    txtstream.WriteLine("<tr><th>"    &    prop.Name    &    "</th><td>"    &
GetValue(prop.Name, obj) & "</td></tr>")
    next
txtstream.WriteLine("</table>")
txtstream.WriteLine("</body>")
txtstream.WriteLine("</html>")
txtstream.close
```

For Multi Line Vertical

```
txtstream.WriteLine("<html>")
txtstream.WriteLine("<head>")
txtstream.WriteLine("<HTA:APPLICATION ")
txtstream.WriteLine("ID = ""Process"" ")
txtstream.WriteLine("APPLICATIONNAME = ""Process"" ")
txtstream.WriteLine("SCROLL = ""yes"" ")
txtstream.WriteLine("SINGLEINSTANCE = ""yes"" ")
txtstream.WriteLine("WINDOWSTATE = ""maximize"" >")

txtstream.WriteLine("<style type='text/css'>")
txtstream.WriteLine("th")
txtstream.WriteLine("{")
txtstream.WriteLine("   COLOR: darkred;")
```

```
txtstream.WriteLine("    BACKGROUND-COLOR: white;")
txtstream.WriteLine("    FONT-FAMILY:font-family: Cambria, serif;")
txtstream.WriteLine("    FONT-SIZE: 12px;")
txtstream.WriteLine("    text-align: left;")
txtstream.WriteLine("    white-Space: nowrap;")
txtstream.WriteLine("}")
txtstream.WriteLine("td")
txtstream.WriteLine("{")
txtstream.WriteLine("    COLOR: navy;")
txtstream.WriteLine("    BACKGROUND-COLOR: white;")
txtstream.WriteLine("    FONT-FAMILY: font-family: Cambria, serif;")
txtstream.WriteLine("    FONT-SIZE: 12px;")
txtstream.WriteLine("    text-align: left;")
txtstream.WriteLine("    white-Space: nowrap;")
txtstream.WriteLine("}")
txtstream.WriteLine("</style>")
txtstream.WriteLine("<title>Win32_Process</title>")
txtstream.WriteLine("</head>")
txtstream.WriteLine("<body>")
```

Use this if you want to create a border around your table:
```
txtstream.WriteLine("<table Border='1' cellpadding='1' cellspacing='1'>")
```

Use this if you don't want to create a border around your table:
```
txtstream.WriteLine("<table Border='0' cellpadding='1' cellspacing='1'>")
Set obj = objs.ItemIndex(0)
for each prop in obj.Properties_
   txtstream.WriteLine("<tr><th>" & prop.Name & "</th>")
   for each obj in objs
     txtstream.WriteLine("<td>" & GetValue(prop.Name, obj) & "</td>")
   next
   txtstream.WriteLine("</tr>")
Next
```

```
txtstream.WriteLine("</table>")
txtstream.WriteLine("</body>")
txtstream.WriteLine("</html>")
txtstream.close
```

HTML Code

elow, is the code for HTML. The getValue function is in Appendix B.

```
Set ws = CreateObject("WScript.Shell")
Set fso = CreateObject("Scripting.FileSystemObject")
Set      txtstream      =      fso.OpenTextFile(ws.CurrentDirectory      +
"\Win32_Process.html", 2, true, -2)
```

For Single Line Horizontal

```
txtstream.WriteLine("<html>")
txtstream.WriteLine("<head>")
txtstream.WriteLine("<style type='text/css'>")
txtstream.WriteLine("th")
txtstream.WriteLine("{")
txtstream.WriteLine("    COLOR: darkred;")
txtstream.WriteLine("    BACKGROUND-COLOR: white;")
txtstream.WriteLine("    FONT-FAMILY:font-family: Cambria, serif;")
txtstream.WriteLine("    FONT-SIZE: 12px;")
txtstream.WriteLine("    text-align: left;")
txtstream.WriteLine("    white-Space: nowrap;")
txtstream.WriteLine("}")
```

```
txtstream.WriteLine("td")
txtstream.WriteLine("{")
txtstream.WriteLine("    COLOR: navy;")
txtstream.WriteLine("    BACKGROUND-COLOR: white;")
txtstream.WriteLine("    FONT-FAMILY: font-family: Cambria, serif;")
txtstream.WriteLine("    FONT-SIZE: 12px;")
txtstream.WriteLine("    text-align: left;")
txtstream.WriteLine("    white-Space: nowrap;")
txtstream.WriteLine("}")
txtstream.WriteLine("</style>")
txtstream.WriteLine("<title>Win32_Process</title>")
txtstream.WriteLine("</head>")
txtstream.WriteLine("<body>")
```

Use this if you want to create a border around your table:
```
txtstream.WriteLine("<table Border='1' cellpadding='1' cellspacing='1'>")
```

Use this if you don't want to create a border around your table:
```
txtstream.WriteLine("<table Border='0' cellpadding='1' cellspacing='1'>")
Set obj = objs.ItemIndex(0)
txtstream.WriteLine("<tr>")
for each prop in obj.Properties_
    txtstream.WriteLine("<th>" & prop.Name & "</th>")
next
txtstream.WriteLine("</tr>")
txtstream.WriteLine("<tr>")
for each prop in obj.Properties_
    txtstream.WriteLine("<td>" & GetValue(prop.Name, obj) & "</td>")
next
txtstream.WriteLine("</tr>")
txtstream.WriteLine("</table>")
txtstream.WriteLine("</body>")
txtstream.WriteLine("</html>")
```

txtstream.close

For Multi Line Horizontal

```
txtstream.WriteLine(html>")
txtstream.WriteLine("<head>")
txtstream.WriteLine("<style type='text/css'>")
txtstream.WriteLine("th")
txtstream.WriteLine("{")
txtstream.WriteLine("    COLOR: darkred;")
txtstream.WriteLine("    BACKGROUND-COLOR: white;")
txtstream.WriteLine("    FONT-FAMILY:font-family: Cambria, serif;")
txtstream.WriteLine("    FONT-SIZE: 12px;")
txtstream.WriteLine("    text-align: left;")
txtstream.WriteLine("    white-Space: nowrap;")
txtstream.WriteLine("}")
txtstream.WriteLine("td")
txtstream.WriteLine("{")
txtstream.WriteLine("    COLOR: navy;")
txtstream.WriteLine("    BACKGROUND-COLOR: white;")
txtstream.WriteLine("    FONT-FAMILY: font-family: Cambria, serif;")
txtstream.WriteLine("    FONT-SIZE: 12px;")
txtstream.WriteLine("    text-align: left;")
txtstream.WriteLine("    white-Space: nowrap;")
txtstream.WriteLine("}")
txtstream.WriteLine("</style>")
txtstream.WriteLine("<title>Win32_Process</title>")
txtstream.WriteLine("</head>")
txtstream.WriteLine("<body>")
```

Use this if you want to create a border around your table:
```
txtstream.WriteLine("<table Border='1' cellpadding='1' cellspacing='1'>")
```

Use this if you don't want to create a border around your table:
txtstream.WriteLine("<table Border='0' cellpadding='1' cellspacing='1'>")

Set obj = objs.ItemIndex(0)
txtstream.WriteLine("<tr>")
for each prop in obj.Properties_
    txtstream.WriteLine("<th>" & prop.Name & "</th>")
next
txtstream.WriteLine("</tr>")
for each obj in objs
    txtstream.WriteLine("<tr>")
    for each prop in obj.Properties_
        txtstream.WriteLine("<td>" & GetValue(prop.Name, obj) & "</td>")
    next
    txtstream.WriteLine("</tr>")
Next
txtstream.WriteLine("</table>")
txtstream.WriteLine("</body>")
txtstream.WriteLine("</html>")
txtstream.close

For Single Line Vertical

txtstream.WriteLine("<html>")
txtstream.WriteLine("<head>")
txtstream.WriteLine("<style type='text/css'>")
txtstream.WriteLine("th")
txtstream.WriteLine("{")
txtstream.WriteLine("   COLOR: darkred;")
txtstream.WriteLine("   BACKGROUND-COLOR: white;")
txtstream.WriteLine("   FONT-FAMILY:font-family: Cambria, serif;")
txtstream.WriteLine("   FONT-SIZE: 12px;")

```
txtstream.WriteLine("    text-align: left;")
txtstream.WriteLine("    white-Space: nowrap;")
txtstream.WriteLine("}")
txtstream.WriteLine("td")
txtstream.WriteLine("{")
txtstream.WriteLine("    COLOR: navy;")
txtstream.WriteLine("    BACKGROUND-COLOR: white;")
txtstream.WriteLine("    FONT-FAMILY: font-family: Cambria, serif;")
txtstream.WriteLine("    FONT-SIZE: 12px;")
txtstream.WriteLine("    text-align: left;")
txtstream.WriteLine("    white-Space: nowrap;")
txtstream.WriteLine("}")
txtstream.WriteLine("</style>")
txtstream.WriteLine("<title>Win32_Process</title>")
txtstream.WriteLine("</head>")
txtstream.WriteLine("<body>")
```

Use this if you want to create a border around your table:
```
txtstream.WriteLine("<table Border='1' cellpadding='1' cellspacing='1'>")
```

Use this if you don't want to create a border around your table:
```
txtstream.WriteLine("<table Border='0' cellpadding='1' cellspacing='1'>")
```

```
Set obj = objs.ItemIndex(0)
for each prop in obj.Properties_
    txtstream.WriteLine("<tr><th>" & prop.Name & "</th><td>" &
GetValue(prop.Name, obj) & "</td></tr>")
    next
    txtstream.WriteLine("</table>")
    txtstream.WriteLine("</body>")
    txtstream.WriteLine("</html>")
    txtstream.close
```

For Multi Line Vertical

```
txtstream.WriteLine("<html>")
txtstream.WriteLine("<head>")
txtstream.WriteLine("<style type='text/css'>")
txtstream.WriteLine("th")
txtstream.WriteLine("{")
txtstream.WriteLine("   COLOR: darkred;")
txtstream.WriteLine("   BACKGROUND-COLOR: white;")
txtstream.WriteLine("   FONT-FAMILY:font-family: Cambria, serif;")
txtstream.WriteLine("   FONT-SIZE: 12px;")
txtstream.WriteLine("   text-align: left;")
txtstream.WriteLine("   white-Space: nowrap;")
txtstream.WriteLine("}")
txtstream.WriteLine("td")
txtstream.WriteLine("{")
txtstream.WriteLine("   COLOR: navy;")
txtstream.WriteLine("   BACKGROUND-COLOR: white;")
txtstream.WriteLine("   FONT-FAMILY: font-family: Cambria, serif;")
txtstream.WriteLine("   FONT-SIZE: 12px;")
txtstream.WriteLine("   text-align: left;")
txtstream.WriteLine("   white-Space: nowrap;")
txtstream.WriteLine("}")
txtstream.WriteLine("</style>")
txtstream.WriteLine("<title>Win32_Process</title>")
txtstream.WriteLine("</head>")
txtstream.WriteLine("<body>")
```

Use this if you want to create a border around your table:
```
txtstream.WriteLine("<table Border='1' cellpadding='1' cellspacing='1'>")
```

Use this if you don't want to create a border around your table:
```
txtstream.WriteLine("<table Border='0' cellpadding='1' cellspacing='1'>")
Set obj = objs.ItemIndex(0)
```

```
for each prop in obj.Properties_
    txtstream.WriteLine("<tr><th>" & prop.Name & "</th>")
    for each obj in objs
        txtstream.WriteLine("<td>" & GetValue(prop.Name, obj) & "</td>")
    next
    txtstream.WriteLine("</tr>")
Next
txtstream.WriteLine("</table>")
txtstream.WriteLine("</body>")
txtstream.WriteLine("</html>")
txtstream.close
```

Text Delimited File Examples
Text files can be databases, too

Below, are code samples for creating various types of delimited files. The getValue function is in Appendix B.

Colon

```
Dim tempstr
tempstr = ""
Set ws = CreateObject("WScript.Shell")
Set fso = CreateObject("Scripting.FileSystemObject")
Set txtstream = fso.OpenTextFile(ws.CurrentDirectory + "\Win32_Process.txt"
, 2, true, -2)
```

HORIZONTAL

```
Set obj = objs.ItemIndex(0)
For Each prop in obj.Properties_
    if(tempstr <> "")
```

```
      tempstr = tempstr + ":"
   end if
   tempstr = tempstr + prop.Name
Next
txtstream.WriteLine(Tempstr)
for each obj in objs
   For Each prop in obj.Properties_
      if(tempstr <> "")
         tempstr = tempstr  + ":"
      end if
      tempstr = tempstr + chr(34) + GetValue(prop.Name, obj) + chr(34)
   Next
   txtstream.WriteLine(Tempstr)
   tempstr = ""
Next
```

VERTICAL

```
Set obj = objs.ItemIndex(0)
For Each prop in obj.Properties_
   tempstr = prop.Name
   For Each obj in objs
      if(tempstr <> "")
         tempstr = tempstr  + ":"
      end if
      tempstr = tempstr + chr(34) + GetValue(prop.Name, obj) + chr(34)
   Next
   txtstream.WriteLine(Tempstr)
   tempstr = ""
Next
```

Comma Delimited

```
Dim tempstr
tempstr = ""
Set ws = CreateObject("WScript.Shell")
Set fso = CreateObject("Scripting.FileSystemObject")
Set txtstream = fso.OpenTextFile(ws.CurrentDirectory + "\Win32_Process.csv"
, 2, true, -2)
```

HORIZONTAL

```
Set obj = objs.ItemIndex(0)
For Each prop in obj.Properties_
   if(tempstr <> "")
      tempstr = tempstr + ","
   end if
   tempstr = tempstr + prop.Name
Next
txtstream.WriteLine(Tempstr)
for each obj in objs
   For Each prop in obj.Properties_
      if(tempstr <> "")
         tempstr = tempstr  + ","
      end if
      tempstr = tempstr + chr(34) + GetValue(prop.Name, obj) + chr(34)
   Next
   txtstream.WriteLine(Tempstr)
   tempstr = ""
Next
```

```
Set obj = objs.ItemIndex(0)
For Each prop in obj.Properties_
   tempstr = prop.Name
   For Each obj in objs
      if(tempstr <> "")
         tempstr = tempstr  + ","
      end if
      tempstr = tempstr + chr(34) + GetValue(prop.Name, obj) + chr(34)
   Next
   txtstream.WriteLine(Tempstr)
   tempstr = ""
Next
txtstream.Close
```

Exclamation

```
Dim tempstr
tempstr = ""
Set ws = CreateObject("WScript.Shell")
Set fso =  CreateObject("Scripting.FileSystemObject")
```

```
Set txtstream = fso.OpenTextFile(ws.CurrentDirectory + "\Win32_Process.txt",
2, true, -2)
```

HORIZONTAL

```
Set obj = objs.ItemIndex(0)
For Each prop in obj.Properties_
    if(tempstr <> "")
        tempstr = tempstr + "!"
    end if
    tempstr = tempstr + prop.Name
Next
txtstream.WriteLine(Tempstr)
for each obj in objs
    For Each prop in obj.Properties_
        if(tempstr <> "")
            tempstr = tempstr  + "!"
        end if
        tempstr = tempstr + chr(34) + GetValue(prop.Name, obj) + chr(34)
    Next
    txtstream.WriteLine(Tempstr)
    tempstr = ""
Next
```

VERTICAL

```
Set obj = objs.ItemIndex(0)
For Each prop in obj.Properties_
    tempstr = prop.Name
```

```
    For Each obj in objs
       if(tempstr <> "")
          tempstr = tempstr  + "!"
       end if
       tempstr = tempstr + chr(34) + GetValue(prop.Name, obj) + chr(34)
    Next
    txtstream.WriteLine(Tempstr)
    tempstr = ""
  Next
```

SEMI COLON

```
  Dim tempstr
  tempstr = ""
  Set ws = CreateObject("WScript.Shell")
  Set fso =  CreateObject("Scripting.FileSystemObject")
  Set txtstream = fso.OpenTextFile(ws.CurrentDirectory + "\Win32_Process.txt",
2, true, -2)
```

HORIZONTAL

```
  Set obj = objs.ItemIndex(0)
  For Each prop in obj.Properties_
     if(tempstr <> "")
        tempstr = tempstr + ";"
     end if
     tempstr = tempstr + prop.Name
  Next
  txtstream.WriteLine(Tempstr)
```

```
for each obj in objs
   For Each prop in obj.Properties_
      if(tempstr <> "")
         tempstr = tempstr  + ";"
      end if
      tempstr = tempstr + chr(34) + GetValue(prop.Name, obj) + chr(34)
   Next
   txtstream.WriteLine(Tempstr)
   tempstr = ""
Next
```

VERTICAL

```
Set obj = objs.ItemIndex(0)
For Each prop in obj.Properties_
   tempstr = prop.Name
   For Each obj in objs
      if(tempstr <> "")
         tempstr = tempstr  + ";"
      end if
      tempstr = tempstr + chr(34) + GetValue(prop.Name, obj) + chr(34)
   Next
   txtstream.WriteLine(Tempstr)
   tempstr = ""
Next
```

Tab Delimited

```
Dim tempstr
```

```
tempstr = ""
Set ws = CreateObject("WScript.Shell")
Set fso = CreateObject("Scripting.FileSystemObject")
Set txtstream = fso.OpenTextFile(ws.CurrentDirectory + "\Win32_Process.txt",
2, true, -2)
```

HORIZONTAL

```
Set obj = objs.ItemIndex(0)
For Each prop in obj.Properties_
   if(tempstr <> "")
      tempstr = tempstr + vbtab
   end if
   tempstr = tempstr + prop.Name
Next
txtstream.WriteLine(Tempstr)
for each obj in objs
   For Each prop in obj.Properties_
      if(tempstr <> "")
         tempstr = tempstr  + vbtab
      end if
      tempstr = tempstr + chr(34) + GetValue(prop.Name, obj) + chr(34)
   Next
   txtstream.WriteLine(Tempstr)
   tempstr = ""
Next
```

VERTICAL

```
Set obj = objs.ItemIndex(0)
For Each prop in obj.Properties_
   tempstr = prop.Name
   For Each obj in objs
     if(tempstr <> "")
        tempstr = tempstr + vbtab
     end if
     tempstr = tempstr + chr(34) + GetValue(prop.Name, obj) + chr(34)
   Next
   txtstream.WriteLine(Tempstr)
   tempstr = ""
Next
```

Tilde Delimited

```
Dim tempstr
tempstr = ""
Set ws = CreateObject("WScript.Shell")
Set fso = CreateObject("Scripting.FileSystemObject")
Set txtstream = fso.OpenTextFile(ws.CurrentDirectory + "\Win32_Process.txt",
2, true, -2)
```

HORIZONTAL

```
Set obj = objs.ItemIndex(0)
For Each prop in obj.Properties_
   if(tempstr <> "")
     tempstr = tempstr + "~"
   end if
```

```
      tempstr = tempstr + prop.Name
Next
txtstream.WriteLine(Tempstr)
for each obj in objs
   For Each prop in obj.Properties_
      if(tempstr <> "")
         tempstr = tempstr  + "~"
      end if
      tempstr = tempstr + chr(34) + GetValue(prop.Name, obj) + chr(34)
   Next
   txtstream.WriteLine(Tempstr)
   tempstr = ""
Next
```

VERTICAL

```
Set obj = objs.ItemIndex(0)
For Each prop in obj.Properties_
   tempstr = prop.Name
   For Each obj in objs
      if(tempstr <> "~")
         tempstr = tempstr  + vbtab
      end if
      tempstr = tempstr + chr(34) + GetValue(prop.Name, obj) + chr(34)
   Next
   txtstream.WriteLine(Tempstr)
   tempstr = ""
Next
```

THE XML FILES

Because they are out there

WELL, I THOUGHT IT WAS CATCHY. Below, are examples of different types of XML that can be used with the MSDAOSP and MSPERSIST Providers. Element XML as a standalone -no XSL referenced – can be used with the MSDAOSP Provider and Schema XML can be used with MSPersist.

Element XML

```
Set ws = CreateObject("WScript.Shell")
Set fso = CreateObject("Scripting.FileSystemObject")
Set txtstream = fso.OpenTextFile(ws.CurrentDirectory + "\Win32_Process.xml", 2, true, -2)
txtstream.WriteLine("<?xml version='1.0' encoding='iso-8859-1'?>")
txtstream.WriteLine("<data>")
for each obj in objs
    txtstream.WriteLine("<" + Tablename + ">")
    for each prop in obj.Properties_
        txtstream.WriteLine("<" + prop.Name + ">" + GetValue(prop.Name, obj) + "</" + prop.Name + ">")
    next
```

```
        txtstream.WriteLine("</" + Tablename + ">")
    next
    txtstream.WriteLine("</data>")
    txtstream.close
```

WMI to Element XML For XSL

```
    Set ws = CreateObject("WScript.Shell")
    Set fso = CreateObject("Scripting.FileSystemObject")
    Set     txtstream     =     fso.OpenTextFile(ws.CurrentDirectory     +
"\Win32_Process.xml", 2, true, -2)
    txtstream.WriteLine("<?xml version='1.0' encoding='iso-8859-1'?>")
    txtstream.WriteLine("<?xml-stylesheet     type='Text/xsl'     href="""     +
ws.CurrentDirectory + "\Win32_Process.xsl""?>")
    txtstream.WriteLine("<data>")
    for each obj in objs
        txtstream.WriteLine("<" + Tablename + ">")
        for each prop in obj.Properties_
            txtstream.WriteLine("<" + prop.Name + ">" + GetValue(prop.Name, obj)+
"</" + prop.Name + ">")
        next
        txtstream.WriteLine("</" + Tablename + ">")
    next
    txtstream.WriteLine("</data>")
    txtstream.close
```

SCHEMA XML

```
    Set ws = CreateObject("WScript.Shell")
    Set fso = CreateObject("Scripting.FileSystemObject")
```

```
    Set     txtstream    =        fso.OpenTextFile(ws.CurrentDirectory        +
"\Win32_Process.xml", 2, true, -2)
    txtstream.WriteLine("<?xml version='1.0' encoding='iso-8859-1'?>")
    txtstream.WriteLine("<data>")
    for each obj in objs
        txtstream.WriteLine("<" + Tablename + ">")
        for each prop in obj.Properties_
            txtstream.WriteLine("<" + prop.Name + ">" + GetValue(prop.Name, obj)+
"</" + prop.Name + ">")
        next
        txtstream.WriteLine("</" + Tablename + ">")
    next
    txtstream.WriteLine("</data>")
    txtstream.close

    Set rs1 = CreateObject("ADODB.Recordset")
    rs1.ActiveConnection         =          "Provider=MSDAOSP;        Data
Source=msxml2.DSOControl"
    rs1.Open(ws.CurrentDirectory + "\Win32_Process.xml")

    if(fso.FileExists(ws.CurrentDirectory    +    "\Win32_Process_Schema.xml")    =
true)
        fso.DeleteFile(ws.CurrentDirectory + "\Win32_Process_Schema.xml")
    end if
    rs.Save(ws.CurrentDirectory + "\Win32_Process_Schema.xml, 1)
```

EXCEL
Three ways to get the job done

THERE ARE THREE WAYS TO PUT DATA INTO EXCEL. CREATE A COMA DELIMITED FILE AND THEN USE WS.RUN, THROUGH AUTOMATION AND BY CREATING A PHYSICAL SPREADSHEET. Below are examples of doing exactly that.

Using the comma delimited file

```
Dim tempstr
tempstr = ""
Set ws = CreateObject("WScript.Shell")
Set fso = CreateObject("Scripting.FileSystemObject")
Set txtstream = fso.OpenTextFile(ws.CurrentDirectory + "\Win32_Process.csv", 2, true, -2)
```

HORIZONTAL

```
Set obj = objs.ItemIndex(0)
For Each prop in obj.Properties_
```

```
    if(tempstr <> "")
       tempstr = tempstr + ","
    end if
    tempstr = tempstr + prop.Name
Next
txtstream.WriteLine(Tempstr)
for each obj in objs
    For Each prop in obj.Properties_
       if(tempstr <> "")
          tempstr = tempstr  + ","
       end if
       tempstr = tempstr + chr(34) + GetValue(prop.Name, obj) + chr(34)
    Next
    txtstream.WriteLine(Tempstr)
    tempstr = ""
Next
txtstream.close
ws.Run(ws.CurrentDirectory + "\Win32_Process.csv")
```

VERTICAL

```
Set obj = objs.ItemIndex(0)
For Each prop in obj.Properties_
    tempstr = prop.Name
    For Each obj in objs
       if(tempstr <> "")
          tempstr = tempstr  + ","
       end if
       tempstr = tempstr + chr(34) + GetValue(prop.Name, obj) + chr(34)
    Next
    txtstream.WriteLine(Tempstr)
```

```
    tempstr = ""
Next
txtstream.Close

ws.Run(ws.CurrentDirectory + "\Win32_Process.csv")
```

Excel Automation

```
Dim x
Dim y

Set oExcel = CreateObject("Excel.Application")
oExcel.Visible = True
Set wb = oExcel.Workbooks.Add()
Ser ws = wb.Worksheets(0)
ws.Name = Tablename
y=2
x=1
Set obj = objs.ItemIndex(0)
for each prop in obj.Properties_
   ws.Cells.Item(1, x) = prop.Name
   x=x+1
next
x=1
for each obj in objs
   for each prop in obj.Properties_)
      ws.Cells.Item(y, x) = GetValue(prop.Name, obj)
      x=x+1
   next
```

```
    x= 1
    y=y+1
next
ws.Columns.HorizontalAlignment = -4131
ws.Columns.AutoFit()
```

FOR A VERTICAL VIEW

```
Dim x
Dim y


Set oExcel = CreateObject("Excel.Application")
oExcel.Visible = True
Set wb = oExcel.Workbooks.Add()
Set ws = wb.Worksheets(0)
ws.Name = Tablename
y=2
x=1
Set obj = objs.ItemIndex(0)
for each prop in obj.Properties_
    ws.Cells.Item(x, 1) = prop.Name
    x=x+1
next
x=1
for each obj in objs
    for each prop in obj.Properties_)
        ws.Cells.Item(x, y) = GetValue(prop.Name, obj)
        x=x+1
    next
    x= 1
    y=y+1
```

```
next
ws.Columns.HorizontalAlignment = -4131
ws.Columns.AutoFit()
```

Using A Spreadsheet

```
Set ws = CreateObject("WScript.Shell")
Set fso = CreateObject("Scripting.FileSystemObject")
Set txtstream = fso.OpenTextFile(ws.CurrentDirectory + "\\ProcessExcel.xml",
2, True, -2)
txtstream.WriteLine("<?xml version='1.0'?>")
txtstream.WriteLine("<?mso-application progid='Excel.Sheet'?>")
txtstream.WriteLine("<Workbook          xmlns='urn:schemas-microsoft-
com:office:spreadsheet'      xmlns:o='urn:schemas-microsoft-com:office:office'
xmlns:x='urn:schemas-microsoft-com:office:excel'      xmlns:ss='urn:schemas-
microsoft-com:office:spreadsheet'       xmlns:html='http://www.w3.org/TR/REC-
html40'>")
    txtstream.WriteLine("      <DocumentProperties      xmlns='urn:schemas-
microsoft-com:office:office'>")
    txtstream.WriteLine("               <Author>Windows User</Author>")
    txtstream.WriteLine("               <LastAuthor>Windows
User</LastAuthor>")
    txtstream.WriteLine("               <Created>2007-11-
27T19:36:16Z</Created>")
    txtstream.WriteLine("               <Version>12.00</Version>")
    txtstream.WriteLine("      </DocumentProperties>")
    txtstream.WriteLine("      <ExcelWorkbook          xmlns='urn:schemas-
microsoft-com:office:excel'>")
    txtstream.WriteLine("
    <WindowHeight>11835</WindowHeight>")
    txtstream.WriteLine("
    <WindowWidth>18960</WindowWidth>")
```

```
txtstream.WriteLine("                        <WindowTopX>120</WindowTopX>")
txtstream.WriteLine("                        <WindowTopY>135</WindowTopY>")
txtstream.WriteLine("
    <ProtectStructure>False</ProtectStructure>")
txtstream.WriteLine("
    <ProtectWindows>False</ProtectWindows>")
txtstream.WriteLine("        </ExcelWorkbook>")
txtstream.WriteLine("        <Styles>")
txtstream.WriteLine("                    <Style                ss:ID='Default'
ss:Name='Normal'>")
txtstream.WriteLine("                        <Alignment
ss:Vertical='Bottom'/>")
txtstream.WriteLine("                        <Borders/>")
txtstream.WriteLine("                        <Font    ss:FontName='Calibri'
x:Family='Swiss' ss:Size='11' ss:Color='#000000'/>")
txtstream.WriteLine("                        <Interior/>")
txtstream.WriteLine("                        <NumberFormat/>")
txtstream.WriteLine("                        <Protection/>")
txtstream.WriteLine("                    </Style>")
txtstream.WriteLine("                <Style ss:ID='s62'>")
txtstream.WriteLine("                        <Borders/>")
txtstream.WriteLine("                        <Font    ss:FontName='Calibri'
x:Family='Swiss' ss:Size='11' ss:Color='#000000' ss:Bold='1'/>")
txtstream.WriteLine("                    </Style>")
txtstream.WriteLine("                <Style ss:ID='s63'>")
txtstream.WriteLine("                        <Alignment
ss:Horizontal='Left' ss:Vertical='Bottom' ss:Indent='2'/>")
txtstream.WriteLine("                        <Font  ss:FontName='Verdana'
x:Family='Swiss' ss:Size='7.7' ss:Color='#000000'/>")
txtstream.WriteLine("                    </Style>")
txtstream.WriteLine("   </Styles>")
txtstream.WriteLine("<Worksheet ss:Name='Process'>")
```

```
        txtstream.WriteLine("          <Table    x:FullColumns='1'    x:FullRows='1'
ss:DefaultRowHeight='24.9375'>")
        txtstream.WriteLine("            <Column ss:AutoFitWidth='1' ss:Width='82.5'
ss:Span='5'/>")
    For Each obj in objs
        txtstream.WriteLine("    <Row ss:AutoFitHeight='0'>")
        For Each prop in obj.Properties_
            txtstream.WriteLine("                    <Cell  ss:StyleID='s62'><Data
ss:Type='String'>" + prop.Name + "</Data></Cell>")
        Next
        txtstream.WriteLine("    </Row>")
        Exit for
    Next


    For Each obj in objs
        txtstream.WriteLine("    <Row ss:AutoFitHeight='0' ss:Height='13.5'>")
        for Each prop in obj.Properties_
            txtstream.WriteLine("      <Cell><Data ss:Type='String'><![CDATA[" +
GetValue(prop.Name, obj) + "]]></Data></Cell>")
        Next
        txtstream.WriteLine("    </Row>")
    Next
    txtstream.WriteLine("  </Table>")
    txtstream.WriteLine("          <WorksheetOptions        xmlns='urn:schemas-
microsoft-com:office:excel'>")
    txtstream.WriteLine("              <PageSetup>")
    txtstream.WriteLine("                <Header x:Margin='0.3'/>")
    txtstream.WriteLine("                <Footer x:Margin='0.3'/>")
    txtstream.WriteLine("                <PageMargins x:Bottom='0.75'
x:Left='0.7' x:Right='0.7' x:Top='0.75'/>")
    txtstream.WriteLine("              </PageSetup>")
    txtstream.WriteLine("              <Unsynced/>")
```

```
txtstream.WriteLine("                    <Print>")
txtstream.WriteLine("                         <FitHeight>0</FitHeight>")
txtstream.WriteLine("                         <ValidPrinterInfo/>")
txtstream.WriteLine("
    <HorizontalResolution>600</HorizontalResolution>")
txtstream.WriteLine("
    <VerticalResolution>600</VerticalResolution>")
txtstream.WriteLine("                    </Print>")
txtstream.WriteLine("                 <Selected/>")
txtstream.WriteLine("                 <Panes>")
txtstream.WriteLine("                      <Pane>")
txtstream.WriteLine("
    <Number>3</Number>")
txtstream.WriteLine("
    <ActiveRow>9</ActiveRow>")
txtstream.WriteLine("
    <ActiveCol>7</ActiveCol>")
txtstream.WriteLine("                           </Pane>")
txtstream.WriteLine("                  </Panes>")
txtstream.WriteLine("
    <ProtectObjects>False</ProtectObjects>")
txtstream.WriteLine("
    <ProtectScenarios>False</ProtectScenarios>")
txtstream.WriteLine("         </WorksheetOptions>")
txtstream.WriteLine("</Worksheet>")
txtstream.WriteLine("</Workbook>")
txtstream.Close()
ws.Run(ws.CurrentDirectory + "\ProcessExcel.xml")
```

XSL
The end of the line

BELOW ARE WAYS YOU CAN CREATE XSL FILES TO RENDER YOU XML. Viewer discretion is advised.

```
Set ws = CreateObject("WScript.Shell")
Set fso = CreateObject("Scripting.FileSystemObject")
Set txtstream = fso.OpenTextFile(ws.CurrentDirectory + "\Process.xsl", 2, true,
-2)
```

SINGLE LINE HORIZONTAL

```
txtstream.WriteLine("<?xml version=""1.0" " encoding=""UTF-8" "?>")
txtstream.WriteLine("<xsl:stylesheet                version=""1.0""
xmlns:xsl=""http://www.w3.org/1999/XSL/Transform" ">")
txtstream.WriteLine("<xsl:template match=""/"">")
txtstream.WriteLine("<html>")
```

```
txtstream.WriteLine("<head>")
txtstream.WriteLine("<title>Products</title>")
txtstream.WriteLine("<style type='text/css'>")
txtstream.WriteLine("th")
txtstream.WriteLine("{")
txtstream.WriteLine("    COLOR: darkred;")
txtstream.WriteLine("    BACKGROUND-COLOR: white;")
txtstream.WriteLine("    FONT-FAMILY:font-family: Cambria, serif;")
txtstream.WriteLine("    FONT-SIZE: 12px;")
txtstream.WriteLine("    text-align: left;")
txtstream.WriteLine("    white-Space: nowrap;")
txtstream.WriteLine("}")
txtstream.WriteLine("td")
txtstream.WriteLine("{")
txtstream.WriteLine("    COLOR: navy;")
txtstream.WriteLine("    BACKGROUND-COLOR: white;")
txtstream.WriteLine("    FONT-FAMILY: font-family: Cambria, serif;")
txtstream.WriteLine("    FONT-SIZE: 12px;")
txtstream.WriteLine("    text-align: left;")
txtstream.WriteLine("    white-Space: nowrap;")
txtstream.WriteLine("}")
txtstream.WriteLine("</style>")
txtstream.WriteLine("</head>")
txtstream.WriteLine("<body bgcolor=""#333333" ">")
txtstream.WriteLine("<table colspacing=""3" " colpadding=""3" ">")
Set obj = objs.ItemIndex(0)
txtstream.WriteLine("<tr>")
for each prop in obj.Properties_
    txtstream.WriteLine("<th>" + prop.Name + </th>")
next
txtstream.WriteLine("</tr>")
txtstream.WriteLine("<tr>")
for each prop in obj.Properties_
```

```
        txtstream.WriteLine("<td><xsl:value-of  select=""data/Win32_Process/"  +
prop.Name  + """/></td>")
    next
    txtstream.WriteLine("</tr>")
    txtstream.WriteLine("</table>")
    txtstream.WriteLine("</body>")
    txtstream.WriteLine("</html>")
    txtstream.WriteLine("</xsl:template>")
    txtstream.WriteLine("</xsl:stylesheet>")
    txtstream.Close()
```

For Multi Line Horizontal

```
    txtstream.WriteLine("<?xml version=""1.0" encoding=""UTF-8" "?>")
    txtstream.WriteLine("<xsl:stylesheet                        version=""1.0""
xmlns:xsl=""http://www.w3.org/1999/XSL/Transform" ">")
    txtstream.WriteLine("<xsl:template match=""/"">")
    txtstream.WriteLine("<html>")
    txtstream.WriteLine("<head>")
    txtstream.WriteLine("<title>Products</title>")
    txtstream.WriteLine("<style type='text/css'>")
    txtstream.WriteLine("th")
    txtstream.WriteLine("{")
    txtstream.WriteLine("    COLOR: darkred;")
    txtstream.WriteLine("    BACKGROUND-COLOR: white;")
    txtstream.WriteLine("    FONT-FAMILY:font-family: Cambria, serif;")
    txtstream.WriteLine("    FONT-SIZE: 12px;")
    txtstream.WriteLine("    text-align: left;")
    txtstream.WriteLine("    white-Space: nowrap;")
    txtstream.WriteLine("}")
    txtstream.WriteLine("td")
```

```
txtstream.WriteLine("{")
txtstream.WriteLine("   COLOR: navy;")
txtstream.WriteLine("   BACKGROUND-COLOR: white;")
txtstream.WriteLine("   FONT-FAMILY: font-family: Cambria, serif;")
txtstream.WriteLine("   FONT-SIZE: 12px;")
txtstream.WriteLine("   text-align: left;")
txtstream.WriteLine("   white-Space: nowrap;")
txtstream.WriteLine("}")
txtstream.WriteLine("</style>")
txtstream.WriteLine("</head>")
txtstream.WriteLine("<body bgcolor=""#333333" ">")
txtstream.WriteLine("<table colspacing=""3" " colpadding=""3" ">")


Set obj = objs.ItemIndex(0)
txtstream.WriteLine("<tr>")
for each prop in obj.Properties_
    txtstream.WriteLine("<th>" + prop.Name + </th>")
next
txtstream.WriteLine("</tr>")
txtstream.WriteLine("<xsl:for-each select=""data/Win32_Process"">")
txtstream.WriteLine("<tr>")
for each prop in obj.Properties_
    txtstream.WriteLine("<td><xsl:value-of   select=""   +   prop.Name   +
""/></td>")
next
txtstream.WriteLine("</tr>")
txtstream.WriteLine("</xsl:for-each>")
txtstream.WriteLine("</table>")
txtstream.WriteLine("</body>")
txtstream.WriteLine("</html>")
txtstream.WriteLine("</xsl:template>")
txtstream.WriteLine("</xsl:stylesheet>")
```

```
txtstream.Close()
```

For Single Line Vertical

```
txtstream.WriteLine("<?xml version=""1.0" " encoding=""UTF-8" "?>")
txtstream.WriteLine("<xsl:stylesheet                    version=""1.0""
xmlns:xsl=""http://www.w3.org/1999/XSL/Transform" ">")
txtstream.WriteLine("<xsl:template match=""/"">")
txtstream.WriteLine("<html>")
txtstream.WriteLine("<head>")
txtstream.WriteLine("<title>Products</title>")
txtstream.WriteLine("<style type='text/css'>")
txtstream.WriteLine("th")
txtstream.WriteLine("{")
txtstream.WriteLine("   COLOR: darkred;")
txtstream.WriteLine("   BACKGROUND-COLOR: white;")
txtstream.WriteLine("   FONT-FAMILY:font-family: Cambria, serif;")
txtstream.WriteLine("   FONT-SIZE: 12px;")
txtstream.WriteLine("   text-align: left;")
txtstream.WriteLine("   white-Space: nowrap;")
txtstream.WriteLine("}")
txtstream.WriteLine("td")
txtstream.WriteLine("{")
txtstream.WriteLine("   COLOR: navy;")
txtstream.WriteLine("   BACKGROUND-COLOR: white;")
txtstream.WriteLine("   FONT-FAMILY: font-family: Cambria, serif;")
txtstream.WriteLine("   FONT-SIZE: 12px;")
txtstream.WriteLine("   text-align: left;")
txtstream.WriteLine("   white-Space: nowrap;")
txtstream.WriteLine("}")
txtstream.WriteLine("</style>")
txtstream.WriteLine("</head>")
```

```
txtstream.WriteLine("<body bgcolor=""#333333" ">")
txtstream.WriteLine("<table colspacing=""3" " colpadding=""3" ">")

obj = objs.ItemIndex[0]
for each prop in obj.Properties_
    txtstream.WriteLine("<tr><th>" + prop.Name + </th>")
    txtstream.WriteLine("<td><xsl:value-of select=""data/Win32_Process/" +
prop.Name + """/></td></tr>")
next
txtstream.WriteLine("</table>")
txtstream.WriteLine("</body>")
txtstream.WriteLine("</html>")
txtstream.WriteLine("</xsl:template>")
txtstream.WriteLine("</xsl:stylesheet>")
txtstream.Close()
```

For Multi Line Vertical

```
txtstream.WriteLine("<?xml version=""1.0" " encoding=""UTF-8" "?>")
txtstream.WriteLine("<xsl:stylesheet                        version=""1.0""
xmlns:xsl=""http://www.w3.org/1999/XSL/Transform" ">")
txtstream.WriteLine("<xsl:template match=""/"">")
txtstream.WriteLine("<html>")
txtstream.WriteLine("<head>")
txtstream.WriteLine("<title>Products</title>")
txtstream.WriteLine("<style type='text/css'>")
txtstream.WriteLine("th")
```

```
txtstream.WriteLine("{")
txtstream.WriteLine("   COLOR: darkred;")
txtstream.WriteLine("   BACKGROUND-COLOR: white;")
txtstream.WriteLine("   FONT-FAMILY:font-family: Cambria, serif;")
txtstream.WriteLine("   FONT-SIZE: 12px;")
txtstream.WriteLine("   text-align: left;")
txtstream.WriteLine("   white-Space: nowrap;")
txtstream.WriteLine("}")
txtstream.WriteLine("td")
txtstream.WriteLine("{")
txtstream.WriteLine("   COLOR: navy;")
txtstream.WriteLine("   BACKGROUND-COLOR: white;")
txtstream.WriteLine("   FONT-FAMILY: font-family: Cambria, serif;")
txtstream.WriteLine("   FONT-SIZE: 12px;")
txtstream.WriteLine("   text-align: left;")
txtstream.WriteLine("   white-Space: nowrap;")
txtstream.WriteLine("}")
txtstream.WriteLine("</style>")
txtstream.WriteLine("</head>")
txtstream.WriteLine("<body bgcolor=""#333333" ">")
txtstream.WriteLine("<table colspacing=""3" " colpadding=""3" ">")

txtstream.WriteLine("<tr>")
obj = objs.ItemIndex[0]
for each prop in obj.Properties_
   txtstream.WriteLine("<tr><th>" + prop.Name + </th>")
   txtstream.WriteLine("<td><xsl:for-each select=""data/Win32_Process"">")
   txtstream.WriteLine("<xsl:value-of select=""" + prop.Name + """/></td>")
   txtstream.WriteLine("</xsl:for-each></tr>")
next
txtstream.WriteLine("</table>")
txtstream.WriteLine("</body>")
txtstream.WriteLine("</html>")
```

```
txtstream.WriteLine("</xsl:template>")
txtstream.WriteLine("</xsl:stylesheet>")
txtstream.Close()
```

Stylesheets

The difference between boring and oh, wow!

THE stylesheets in Appendix A, were used to create these web pages. If you find one you like, feel free to use it.

Report:

OrderID	CustomerID	EmployeeID	OrderDate	RequiredDate	ShippedDate	ShipVia	Freight	ShipName	ShipAddress	ShipCity	ShipRegion	ShipPostalCode	ShipCountry
10308	LILAS	1	11/18/1994 00:00:00	12/14/1994 00:00:00	11/18/1994 00:00:00	1	13.73	LILA-Supermercado	Carrera 52 con Ave. Bolívar #65-98 Llano Largo	Barquisimeto	Lara	3508	Venezuela
10309	BONAP	5	11/16/1994 00:00:00	12/28/1994 00:00:00	11/21/1994 00:00:00	1	18.19	Bon app'	12, rue des Bouchers	Marseille		13008	France
10310	HEREP	3	11/17/1994 00:00:00	12/29/1994 00:00:00	11/21/1994 00:00:00	3	12.84	Mère Paillarde	43 rue St. Laurent	Montréal	Québec	H1J 1C3	Canada
10311	WARTH	3	11/18/1994 00:00:00	11/16/1994 00:00:00	11/23/1994 00:00:00	3	0.50	Wartian Herkku	Torikatu 38	Oulu		90110	Finland
10314	VICTE	8	11/21/1994 00:00:00	12/19/1994 00:00:00	11/28/1994 00:00:00	3	8.56	Victuailles en stock	2, rue du Commerce	Lyon		69004	France
10315	HUNGO	7	11/23/1994 00:00:00	12/21/1994 00:00:00	11/24/1994 00:00:00	2	41.21	Hungry Owl All-Night Grocers	8 Johnstown Road	Cork	Co. Cork		Ireland
10316	PRINI	7	11/23/1994 00:00:00	12/21/1994 00:00:00	12/03/1994 00:00:00	3	15.51	Princesa Isabel Vinhos	Estrada da saúde n. 58	Lisboa		1756	Portugal
10317	FRANK	4	11/24/1994 00:00:00	12/22/1994 00:00:00	11/24/1994 00:00:00	3	139.26	Frankenversand	Berliner Platz 43	München		80805	Germany
10318	OLDWO	4	11/21/1994 00:00:00	12/27/1994 00:00:00	11/24/1994 00:00:00	1	84.21	Old World Delicatessen	2743 Bering St.	Anchorage	AK	99508	USA
10319	HEREP	2	11/28/1994 00:00:00	12/08/1994 00:00:00	12/05/1994 00:00:00	1	13.96	Mère Paillarde	43 rue St. Laurent	Montréal	Québec	H1J 1C3	Canada
10320	BONAP	1	11/29/1994 00:00:00	12/27/1994 00:00:00	12/09/1994 00:00:00	3	164.31	Bon app'	12, rue des Bouchers	Marseille		13008	France
10321	SIMOB	7	11/25/1994 00:00:00	12/27/1994 00:00:00	12/09/1994 00:00:00	2	26.73	Simons bistro	Vinbæltet 34	København		1734	Denmark
10322	FRANK	4	11/30/1994 00:00:00	12/24/1994 00:00:00	12/02/1994 00:00:00	1	84.89	Frankenversand	Berliner Platz 43	München		80805	Germany
10340	LEHMS	4	12/01/1994 00:00:00	12/05/1994 00:00:00	12/07/1994 00:00:00	1	113.57	Lehmanns Marktstand	Magazinweg 7	Frankfurt a.M.		60528	Germany
10344	WHITC	4	12/01/1994 00:00:00	12/06/1994 00:00:00	12/06/1994 00:00:00	2	23.29	White Clover Markets	1029 - 12th Ave. S.	Seattle	WA	98124	USA
10345	QUICK	2	12/05/1994 00:00:00	01/02/1995 00:00:00	12/12/1994 00:00:00	2	249.06	QUICK-Stop	Taucherstraße 10	Cunewalde		01307	Germany
10348	SATTC	2	12/06/1994 00:00:00	01/17/1995 00:00:00	12/09/1994 00:00:00	3	142.08	Rattlesnake Canyon Grocery	2817 Milton Dr.	Albuquerque	NM	87110	USA
10349	VINET	3	08/04/1994 00:00:00	06/01/1994 00:00:00	08/16/1994 00:00:00	1	32.38	Vins et alcools Chevalier	59 rue de l'Abbaye	Reims		51100	France
10350	TOMSP	4	08/01/1994 00:00:00	09/16/1994 00:00:00	08/16/1994 00:00:00	1	11.51	Toms Spezialitäten	Luisenstr. 48	Münster		44087	Germany
10351	HANAR	4	08/06/1994 00:00:00	06/05/1994 00:00:00	08/13/1994 00:00:00	2	65.83	Hanari Carnes	Rua do Paço, 67	Rio de Janeiro	RJ	05454-876	Brazil
10352	VICTE	3	08/08/1994 00:00:00	06/03/1994 00:00:00	08/13/1994 00:00:00	1	41.34	Victuailles en stock	2, rue du Commerce	Lyon		69004	France
10353	SUPRD	4	08/06/1994 00:00:00	06/06/1994 00:00:00	08/11/1994 00:00:00	3	21.3	Suprêmes délices	Boulevard Tirou, 255	Charleroi		B-6000	Belgium
10354	HANAR	3	08/31/1994 00:00:00	08/04/1994 00:00:00	08/16/1994 00:00:00	2	36.17	Hanari Carnes	Rua do Paço, 67	Rio de Janeiro	RJ	05454-876	Brazil
10355	CHOPS	3	08/13/1994 00:00:00	09/06/1994 00:00:00	08/23/1994 00:00:00	1	23.36	Chop-suey Chinese	Hauptstr. 31	Bern		3012	Switzerland
10356	RICSU	5	08/11/1994 00:00:00	09/09/1994 00:00:00	08/26/1994 00:00:00	2	149.31	Richter Supermarkt	Starenweg 5	Genève		1204	Switzerland
10357	APOLI	7	08/15/1994 00:00:00	09/12/1994 00:00:00	08/17/1994 00:00:00	1	13.97	Wellington Importadora	Rua do Mercado, 12	Resende	SP	08737-363	Brazil
10358	HILAA	4	08/16/1994 00:00:00	09/13/1994 00:00:00	08/22/1994 00:00:00	3	61.93	HILARIÓN-Abastos	Carrera 22 con Ave. Carlos Soublette #8-35	San Cristóbal	Táchira	5022	Venezuela
10359	ERNSH	1	08/17/1994 00:00:00	09/14/1994 00:00:00	08/23/1994 00:00:00	3	143.51	Ernst Handel	Kirchgasse 6	Graz		8010	Austria
10360	CENTC	4	08/18/1994 00:00:00	06/15/1994 00:00:00	08/23/1994 00:00:00	1	3.25	Centro comercial Moctezuma	Sierras de Granada 9993	México D.F.		05022	Mexico
10361	DITTR	4	08/16/1994 00:00:00	09/20/1994 00:00:00	08/26/1994 00:00:00	1	35.19	Die Wandernde Kuh	Adenauerallee 900	Köln		50739	Germany
10362	QUEDE	4	08/20/1994 00:00:00	09/06/1994 00:00:00	08/08/1994 00:00:00	2	3.35	Que Delícia	Rua da Panificadora, 12	Rio de Janeiro	RJ	02389-673	Brazil

Table

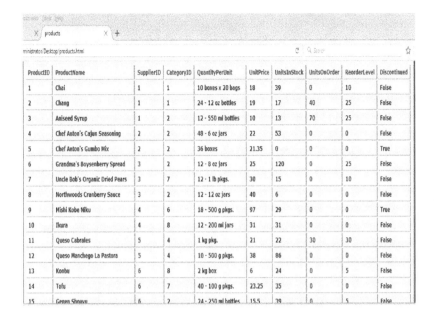

ProductID	ProductName	SupplierID	CategoryID	QuantityPerUnit	UnitPrice	UnitsInStock	UnitsOnOrder	ReorderLevel	Discontinued
1	Chai	1	1	10 boxes x 20 bags	18	39	0	10	False
2	Chang	1	1	24 - 12 oz bottles	19	17	40	25	False
3	Aniseed Syrup	1	2	12 - 550 ml bottles	10	13	70	25	False
4	Chef Anton's Cajun Seasoning	2	2	48 - 6 oz jars	22	53	0	0	False
5	Chef Anton's Gumbo Mix	2	2	36 boxes	21.35	0	0	0	True
6	Grandma's Boysenberry Spread	3	2	12 - 8 oz jars	25	120	0	25	False
7	Uncle Bob's Organic Dried Pears	3	7	12 - 1 lb pkgs.	30	15	0	10	False
8	Northwoods Cranberry Sauce	3	2	12 - 12 oz jars	40	6	0	0	False
9	Mishi Kobe Niku	4	6	18 - 500 g pkgs.	97	29	0	0	True
10	Ikura	4	8	12 - 200 ml jars	31	31	0	0	False
11	Queso Cabrales	5	4	1 kg pkg.	21	22	30	30	False
12	Queso Manchego La Pastora	5	4	10 - 500 g pkgs.	38	86	0	0	False
13	Konbu	6	8	2 kg box	6	24	0	5	False
14	Tofu	6	7	40 - 100 g pkgs.	23.25	35	0	0	False
15	Genen Shouyu	6	2	24 - 250 ml bottles	15.5	39	0	5	False

None:

Availability	BytesPerSector	Capabilities	CapabilityDescriptions	Caption	CompressionMethod	ConfigManagerErrorCode
	512	3, 4, 10	Random Access, Supports Writing, SMART Notification	OCZ-REVODRIVE350 SCSI Disk Device		0
	512	3, 4	Random Access, Supports Writing	NVMe TOSHIBA-RD400		0
	512	3, 4, 10	Random Access, Supports Writing, SMART Notification	TOSHIBA DT01ACA200		0

Black and White

Availability	BytesPerSector	Capabilities	CapabilityDescriptions	Caption	CompressionMethod	ConfigManagerErrorCode	ConfigManagerUserConfig	CreationClassName	DefaultBlockSize	Description	DeviceID	ErrorCleared	ErrorDescription	ErrorMethodology
	512	3, 4, 10	Random Access, Supp	OC		0	FALSE	Win32_DiskDrive		Disk dri				
	512	3, 4	Random Access, Supp	NV		0	FALSE	Win32_DiskDrive		Disk dri				
	512	3, 4, 10	Random Access, Supp	TO		0	FALSE	Win32_DiskDrive		Disk dri				

Colored:

AccountExpires	AuthorizationFlags	BadPasswordCount	Caption	CodePage	Comment	CountryCode	Description
			NT AUTHORITY\SYSTEM				Network login profile settings for SYSTEM on NT AUTHORITY
			NT AUTHORITY\LOCAL SERVICE				Network login profile settings for LOCAL SERVICE on NT AUTHORITY
			NT AUTHORITY\NETWORK SERVICE				Network login profile settings for NETWORK SERVICE on NT AUTHORITY
	0	0	Administrator	0	Built-in account for administering the computer/domain	0	Network login profile settings for on WIN-AIRLOAKMF3B
			NT SERVICE\SSASTELEMETRY				Network login profile settings for SSASTELEMETRY on NT SERVICE
			NT SERVICE\SSISTELEMETRY130				Network login profile settings for SSISTELEMETRY130 on NT SERVICE
			NT SERVICE\SQLTELEMETRY				Network login profile settings for SQLTELEMETRY on NT SERVICE
			NT SERVICE\MSSQLServerOLAPService				Network login profile settings for MSSQLServerOLAPService on NT SERVICE
			NT SERVICE\ReportServer				Network login profile settings for ReportServer on NT SERVICE
			NT SERVICE\MSSQLFDLauncher				Network login profile settings for MSSQLFDLauncher on NT SERVICE
			NT SERVICE\MSSQL$machinpad				Network login profile settings for MSSQL$machinpad on NT SERVICE
			NT SERVICE\SsisDtsServer150				Network login profile settings for SsisDtsServer150 on NT SERVICE
			NT SERVICE\MSSQLSERVER				Network login profile settings for MSSQLSERVER on NT SERVICE
			IIS APPPOOL\Classic .NET AppPool				Network login profile settings for Classic .NET AppPool on IIS APPPOOL
			IIS APPPOOL\.NET v4.5				Network login profile settings for .NET v4.5 on IIS APPPOOL
			IIS APPPOOL\.NET v2.0				Network login profile settings for .NET v2.0 on IIS APPPOOL
			IIS APPPOOL\.NET v4.5 Classic				Network login profile settings for .NET v4.5 Classic on IIS APPPOOL
			IIS APPPOOL\.NET v2.0 Classic				Network login profile settings for .NET v2.0 Classic on IIS APPPOOL

Oscillating:

Availability	BytesPerSector	Capabilities	CapabilityDescriptions	Caption	CompressionMethod	ConfigManagerErrorCode	ConfigManagerUserConfig
	512	3, 4, 10	Random Access, Supports Writing, SMART Notification	OCZ REVODRIVE350 SCSI Disk Device		0	FALSE
	512	3, 4	Random Access, Supports Writing	NVMe TOSHIBA-RD400		0	FALSE
	512	3, 4, 10	Random Access, Supports Writing, SMART Notification	TOSHIBA DT01ACA200		0	FALSE

3D:

Availability	BytesPerSector	Capabilities	CapabilityDescriptions	Caption	CompressionMethod	ConfigManagerErrorCode	ConfigManagerUserConfig	CreationClassName
	512	3, 4, 10	Random Access, Supports Writing, SMART Notification	OCZ REVODRIVE350 SCSI Disk Device		0	FALSE	Win32_DiskDrive
	512	3, 4	Random Access, Supports Writing	NVMe TOSHIBA-RD400		0	FALSE	Win32_DiskDrive
	512	3, 4, 10	Random Access, Supports Writing, SMART Notification	TOSHIBA DT01ACA200		0	FALSE	Win32_DiskDrive

Shadow Box:

Availability	BytesPerSector	Capabilities	CapabilityDescription	Caption	CompressionMethod	ConfigManagerErrorCode	ConfigManagerUserConfig	CreationClassName	DefaultBlockSize
	512	3, 4, 10	Random Access, Supports Writing, SMART Notification	OCZ REVODRIVE350 SCSI Disk Device		0	FALSE	Win32_DiskDrive	
	512	3, 4	Random Access, Supports Writing	NVMe TOSHIBA-RD400		0	FALSE	Win32_DiskDrive	
	512	3, 4, 10	Random Access, Supports Writing, SMART Notification	TOSHIBA DT01ACA200		0	FALSE	Win32_DiskDrive	

Shadow Box Single Line Vertical

BiosCharacteristics	7, 10, 11, 12, 15, 16, 17, 19, 23, 24, 25, 26, 27, 28, 29, 32, 33, 40, 42, 43, 48, 50, 58, 59, 64, 65, 66, 67, 68, 69, 70, 71, 72, 73, 74, 75, 76, 77, 78, 79
BIOSVersion	ALASKA - 1072009, 0504, American Megatrends - 5000C
BuildNumber	
Caption	0504
CodeSet	
CurrentLanguage	en|US|iso8859-1
Description	0504
IdentificationCode	
InstallableLanguages	8
InstallDate	
LanguageEdition	
ListOfLanguages	en|US|iso8859-1, fr|FR|iso8859-1, zh|CN|unicode, , , , ,
Manufacturer	American Megatrends Inc.
Name	0504
OtherTargetOS	
PrimaryBIOS	TRUE

Shadow Box Multi line Vertical

Property	Value 1	Value 2	Value 3
Availability			
BytesPerSector	512	512	512
Capabilities	3, 4, 10	3, 4	3, 4, 10
CapabilityDescriptions	Random Access, Supports Writing, SMART Notification	Random Access, Supports Writing	Random Access, Supports Writing, SMART Notification
Caption	OCZ REVODRIVE350 SCSI Disk Device	NVMe TOSHIBA-RD400	TOSHIBA DT01ACA200
CompressionMethod			
ConfigManagerErrorCode	0	0	0
ConfigManagerUserConfig	FALSE	FALSE	FALSE
CreationClassName	Win32_DiskDrive	Win32_DiskDrive	Win32_DiskDrive
DefaultBlockSize			
Description	Disk drive	Disk drive	Disk drive
DeviceID	\\.\PHYSICALDRIVE2	\\.\PHYSICALDRIVE1	\\.\PHYSICALDRIVE0
ErrorCleared			
ErrorDescription			
ErrorMethodology			
FirmwareRevision	2.50	57CZ4102	MX4OABB0
Index	2	1	0

Stylesheets
Decorating your web pages

BELOW ARE SOME STYLESHEETS I COOKED UP THAT I LIKE AND THINK YOU MIGHT TOO. Don't worry I won't be offended if you take and modify to your hearts delight. Please do!

NONE

```
txtstream.WriteLine("<style type='text/css'>")
txtstream.WriteLine("th")
txtstream.WriteLine("{")
txtstream.WriteLine("    COLOR: white;")
txtstream.WriteLine("}")
txtstream.WriteLine("td")
txtstream.WriteLine("{")
txtstream.WriteLine("    COLOR: white;")
txtstream.WriteLine("}")
txtstream.WriteLine("</style>")
```

BLACK AND WHITE TEXT

```
txtstream.WriteLine("<style type='text/css'>")
txtstream.WriteLine("th")
txtstream.WriteLine("{")
txtstream.WriteLine("   COLOR: white;")
txtstream.WriteLine("   BACKGROUND-COLOR: black;")
txtstream.WriteLine("   FONT-FAMILY:font-family: Cambria, serif;")
txtstream.WriteLine("   FONT-SIZE: 12px;")
txtstream.WriteLine("   text-align: left;")
txtstream.WriteLine("   white-Space: nowrap;")
txtstream.WriteLine("}")
txtstream.WriteLine("td")
txtstream.WriteLine("{")
txtstream.WriteLine("   COLOR: white;")
txtstream.WriteLine("   BACKGROUND-COLOR: black;")
txtstream.WriteLine("   FONT-FAMILY: font-family: Cambria, serif;")
txtstream.WriteLine("   FONT-SIZE: 12px;")
txtstream.WriteLine("   text-align: left;")
txtstream.WriteLine("   white-Space: nowrap;")
txtstream.WriteLine("}")
txtstream.WriteLine("div")
txtstream.WriteLine("{")
txtstream.WriteLine("   COLOR: white;")
txtstream.WriteLine("   BACKGROUND-COLOR: black;")
txtstream.WriteLine("   FONT-FAMILY: font-family: Cambria, serif;")
txtstream.WriteLine("   FONT-SIZE: 10px;")
txtstream.WriteLine("   text-align: left;")
txtstream.WriteLine("   white-Space: nowrap;")
txtstream.WriteLine("}")
txtstream.WriteLine("span")
txtstream.WriteLine("{")
txtstream.WriteLine("   COLOR: white;")
```

```
txtstream.WriteLine("   BACKGROUND-COLOR: black;")
txtstream.WriteLine("   FONT-FAMILY: font-family: Cambria, serif;")
txtstream.WriteLine("   FONT-SIZE: 10px;")
txtstream.WriteLine("   text-align: left;")
txtstream.WriteLine("   white-Space: nowrap;")
txtstream.WriteLine("   display:inline-block;")
txtstream.WriteLine("   width: 100%;")
txtstream.WriteLine("}")
txtstream.WriteLine("textarea")
txtstream.WriteLine("{")
txtstream.WriteLine("   COLOR: white;")
txtstream.WriteLine("   BACKGROUND-COLOR: black;")
txtstream.WriteLine("   FONT-FAMILY: font-family: Cambria, serif;")
txtstream.WriteLine("   FONT-SIZE: 10px;")
txtstream.WriteLine("   text-align: left;")
txtstream.WriteLine("   white-Space: nowrap;")
txtstream.WriteLine("   width: 100%;")
txtstream.WriteLine("}")
txtstream.WriteLine("select")
txtstream.WriteLine("{")
txtstream.WriteLine("   COLOR: white;")
txtstream.WriteLine("   BACKGROUND-COLOR: black;")
txtstream.WriteLine("   FONT-FAMILY: font-family: Cambria, serif;")
txtstream.WriteLine("   FONT-SIZE: 10px;")
txtstream.WriteLine("   text-align: left;")
txtstream.WriteLine("   white-Space: nowrap;")
txtstream.WriteLine("   width: 100%;")
txtstream.WriteLine("}")
txtstream.WriteLine("input")
txtstream.WriteLine("{")
txtstream.WriteLine("   COLOR: white;")
txtstream.WriteLine("   BACKGROUND-COLOR: black;")
txtstream.WriteLine("   FONT-FAMILY: font-family: Cambria, serif;")
```

```
txtstream.WriteLine("   FONT-SIZE: 12px;")
txtstream.WriteLine("   text-align: left;")
txtstream.WriteLine("   display:table-cell;")
txtstream.WriteLine("   white-Space: nowrap;")
txtstream.WriteLine("}")
txtstream.WriteLine("h1 {")
txtstream.WriteLine("color: antiquewhite;")
txtstream.WriteLine("text-shadow: 1px 1px 1px black;")
txtstream.WriteLine("padding: 3px;")
txtstream.WriteLine("text-align: center;")
txtstream.WriteLine("box-shadow: inset 2px 2px 5px rgba(0,0,0,0.5), inset -2px -2px 5px rgba(255,255,255,0.5);")
txtstream.WriteLine("}")
txtstream.WriteLine("</style>")
```

COLORED TEXT

```
txtstream.WriteLine("<style type='text/css'>")
txtstream.WriteLine("th")
txtstream.WriteLine("{")
txtstream.WriteLine("   COLOR: darkred;")
txtstream.WriteLine("   BACKGROUND-COLOR: #eeeeee;")
txtstream.WriteLine("   FONT-FAMILY:font-family: Cambria, serif;")
txtstream.WriteLine("   FONT-SIZE: 12px;")
txtstream.WriteLine("   text-align: left;")
txtstream.WriteLine("   white-Space: nowrap;")
txtstream.WriteLine("}")
txtstream.WriteLine("td")
txtstream.WriteLine("{")
txtstream.WriteLine("   COLOR: navy;")
txtstream.WriteLine("   BACKGROUND-COLOR: #eeeeee;")
txtstream.WriteLine("   FONT-FAMILY: font-family: Cambria, serif;")
txtstream.WriteLine("   FONT-SIZE: 12px;")
```

```
txtstream.WriteLine("    text-align: left;")
txtstream.WriteLine("    white-Space: nowrap;")
txtstream.WriteLine("}")
txtstream.WriteLine("div")
txtstream.WriteLine("{")
txtstream.WriteLine("    COLOR: white;")
txtstream.WriteLine("    BACKGROUND-COLOR: navy;")
txtstream.WriteLine("    FONT-FAMILY: font-family: Cambria, serif;")
txtstream.WriteLine("    FONT-SIZE: 10px;")
txtstream.WriteLine("    text-align: left;")
txtstream.WriteLine("    white-Space: nowrap;")
txtstream.WriteLine("}")
txtstream.WriteLine("span")
txtstream.WriteLine("{")
txtstream.WriteLine("    COLOR: white;")
txtstream.WriteLine("    BACKGROUND-COLOR: navy;")
txtstream.WriteLine("    FONT-FAMILY: font-family: Cambria, serif;")
txtstream.WriteLine("    FONT-SIZE: 10px;")
txtstream.WriteLine("    text-align: left;")
txtstream.WriteLine("    white-Space: nowrap;")
txtstream.WriteLine("    display:inline-block;")
txtstream.WriteLine("    width: 100%;")
txtstream.WriteLine("}")
txtstream.WriteLine("textarea")
txtstream.WriteLine("{")
txtstream.WriteLine("    COLOR: white;")
txtstream.WriteLine("    BACKGROUND-COLOR: navy;")
txtstream.WriteLine("    FONT-FAMILY: font-family: Cambria, serif;")
txtstream.WriteLine("    FONT-SIZE: 10px;")
txtstream.WriteLine("    text-align: left;")
txtstream.WriteLine("    white-Space: nowrap;")
txtstream.WriteLine("    width: 100%;")
txtstream.WriteLine("}")
```

```
txtstream.WriteLine("select")
txtstream.WriteLine("{")
txtstream.WriteLine("    COLOR: white;")
txtstream.WriteLine("    BACKGROUND-COLOR: navy;")
txtstream.WriteLine("    FONT-FAMILY: font-family: Cambria, serif;")
txtstream.WriteLine("    FONT-SIZE: 10px;")
txtstream.WriteLine("    text-align: left;")
txtstream.WriteLine("    white-Space: nowrap;")
txtstream.WriteLine("    width: 100%;")
txtstream.WriteLine("}")
txtstream.WriteLine("input")
txtstream.WriteLine("{")
txtstream.WriteLine("    COLOR: white;")
txtstream.WriteLine("    BACKGROUND-COLOR: navy;")
txtstream.WriteLine("    FONT-FAMILY: font-family: Cambria, serif;")
txtstream.WriteLine("    FONT-SIZE: 12px;")
txtstream.WriteLine("    text-align: left;")
txtstream.WriteLine("    display:table-cell;")
txtstream.WriteLine("    white-Space: nowrap;")
txtstream.WriteLine("}")
txtstream.WriteLine("h1 {")
txtstream.WriteLine("color: antiquewhite;")
txtstream.WriteLine("text-shadow: 1px 1px 1px black;")
txtstream.WriteLine("padding: 3px;")
txtstream.WriteLine("text-align: center;")
txtstream.WriteLine("box-shadow: inset 2px 2px 5px rgba(0,0,0,0.5), inset -2px -2px 5px rgba(255,255,255,0.5);")
txtstream.WriteLine("}")
txtstream.WriteLine("</style>")
```

OSCILLATING ROW COLORS

```
txtstream.WriteLine("<style>")
txtstream.WriteLine("th")
txtstream.WriteLine("{")
txtstream.WriteLine("    COLOR: white;")
txtstream.WriteLine("    BACKGROUND-COLOR: navy;")
txtstream.WriteLine("    FONT-FAMILY:font-family: Cambria, serif;")
txtstream.WriteLine("    FONT-SIZE: 12px;")
txtstream.WriteLine("    text-align: left;")
txtstream.WriteLine("    white-Space: nowrap;")
txtstream.WriteLine("}")
txtstream.WriteLine("td")
txtstream.WriteLine("{")
txtstream.WriteLine("    COLOR: navy;")
txtstream.WriteLine("    FONT-FAMILY: font-family: Cambria, serif;")
txtstream.WriteLine("    FONT-SIZE: 12px;")
txtstream.WriteLine("    text-align: left;")
txtstream.WriteLine("    white-Space: nowrap;")
txtstream.WriteLine("}")
txtstream.WriteLine("div")
txtstream.WriteLine("{")
txtstream.WriteLine("    COLOR: navy;")
txtstream.WriteLine("    FONT-FAMILY: font-family: Cambria, serif;")
txtstream.WriteLine("    FONT-SIZE: 12px;")
txtstream.WriteLine("    text-align: left;")
txtstream.WriteLine("    white-Space: nowrap;")
txtstream.WriteLine("}")
txtstream.WriteLine("span")
txtstream.WriteLine("{")
txtstream.WriteLine("    COLOR: navy;")
txtstream.WriteLine("    FONT-FAMILY: font-family: Cambria, serif;")
txtstream.WriteLine("    FONT-SIZE: 12px;")
txtstream.WriteLine("    text-align: left;")
```

```
txtstream.WriteLine("    white-Space: nowrap;")
txtstream.WriteLine("    width: 100%;")
txtstream.WriteLine("}")
txtstream.WriteLine("textarea")
txtstream.WriteLine("{")
txtstream.WriteLine("    COLOR: navy;")
txtstream.WriteLine("    FONT-FAMILY: font-family: Cambria, serif;")
txtstream.WriteLine("    FONT-SIZE: 12px;")
txtstream.WriteLine("    text-align: left;")
txtstream.WriteLine("    white-Space: nowrap;")
txtstream.WriteLine("    display:inline-block;")
txtstream.WriteLine("    width: 100%;")
txtstream.WriteLine("}")
txtstream.WriteLine("select")
txtstream.WriteLine("{")
txtstream.WriteLine("    COLOR: navy;")
txtstream.WriteLine("    FONT-FAMILY: font-family: Cambria, serif;")
txtstream.WriteLine("    FONT-SIZE: 10px;")
txtstream.WriteLine("    text-align: left;")
txtstream.WriteLine("    white-Space: nowrap;")
txtstream.WriteLine("    display:inline-block;")
txtstream.WriteLine("    width: 100%;")
txtstream.WriteLine("}")
txtstream.WriteLine("input")
txtstream.WriteLine("{")
txtstream.WriteLine("    COLOR: navy;")
txtstream.WriteLine("    FONT-FAMILY: font-family: Cambria, serif;")
txtstream.WriteLine("    FONT-SIZE: 12px;")
txtstream.WriteLine("    text-align: left;")
txtstream.WriteLine("    display:table-cell;")
txtstream.WriteLine("    white-Space: nowrap;")
txtstream.WriteLine("}")
txtstream.WriteLine("h1 {")
```

```
txtstream.WriteLine("color: antiquewhite;")
txtstream.WriteLine("text-shadow: 1px 1px 1px black;")
txtstream.WriteLine("padding: 3px;")
txtstream.WriteLine("text-align: center;")
txtstream.WriteLine("box-shadow: inset 2px 2px 5px rgba(0,0,0,0.5), inset -
2px -2px 5px rgba(255,255,255,0.5);")
txtstream.WriteLine("}")
txtstream.WriteLine("tr:nth-child(even){background-color:#f2f2f2;}")
txtstream.WriteLine("tr:nth-child(odd){background-color:#cccccc;
color:#f2f2f2;}")
txtstream.WriteLine("</style>")
```

GHOST DECORATED

```
txtstream.WriteLine("<style type='text/css'>")
txtstream.WriteLine("th")
txtstream.WriteLine("{")
txtstream.WriteLine("   COLOR: black;")
txtstream.WriteLine("   BACKGROUND-COLOR: white;")
txtstream.WriteLine("   FONT-FAMILY:font-family: Cambria, serif;")
txtstream.WriteLine("   FONT-SIZE: 12px;")
txtstream.WriteLine("   text-align: left;")
txtstream.WriteLine("   white-Space: nowrap;")
txtstream.WriteLine("}")
txtstream.WriteLine("td")
txtstream.WriteLine("{")
txtstream.WriteLine("   COLOR: black;")
txtstream.WriteLine("   BACKGROUND-COLOR: white;")
txtstream.WriteLine("   FONT-FAMILY: font-family: Cambria, serif;")
txtstream.WriteLine("   FONT-SIZE: 12px;")
txtstream.WriteLine("   text-align: left;")
txtstream.WriteLine("   white-Space: nowrap;")
txtstream.WriteLine("}")
```

```
txtstream.WriteLine("div")
txtstream.WriteLine("{")
txtstream.WriteLine("    COLOR: black;")
txtstream.WriteLine("    BACKGROUND-COLOR: white;")
txtstream.WriteLine("    FONT-FAMILY: font-family: Cambria, serif;")
txtstream.WriteLine("    FONT-SIZE: 10px;")
txtstream.WriteLine("    text-align: left;")
txtstream.WriteLine("    white-Space: nowrap;")
txtstream.WriteLine("}")
txtstream.WriteLine("span")
txtstream.WriteLine("{")
txtstream.WriteLine("    COLOR: black;")
txtstream.WriteLine("    BACKGROUND-COLOR: white;")
txtstream.WriteLine("    FONT-FAMILY: font-family: Cambria, serif;")
txtstream.WriteLine("    FONT-SIZE: 10px;")
txtstream.WriteLine("    text-align: left;")
txtstream.WriteLine("    white-Space: nowrap;")
txtstream.WriteLine("    display:inline-block;")
txtstream.WriteLine("    width: 100%;")
txtstream.WriteLine("}")
txtstream.WriteLine("textarea")
txtstream.WriteLine("{")
txtstream.WriteLine("    COLOR: black;")
txtstream.WriteLine("    BACKGROUND-COLOR: white;")
txtstream.WriteLine("    FONT-FAMILY: font-family: Cambria, serif;")
txtstream.WriteLine("    FONT-SIZE: 10px;")
txtstream.WriteLine("    text-align: left;")
txtstream.WriteLine("    white-Space: nowrap;")
txtstream.WriteLine("    width: 100%;")
txtstream.WriteLine("}")
txtstream.WriteLine("select")
txtstream.WriteLine("{")
txtstream.WriteLine("    COLOR: black;")
```

```
txtstream.WriteLine("   BACKGROUND-COLOR: white;")
txtstream.WriteLine("   FONT-FAMILY: font-family: Cambria, serif;")
txtstream.WriteLine("   FONT-SIZE: 10px;")
txtstream.WriteLine("   text-align: left;")
txtstream.WriteLine("   white-Space: nowrap;")
txtstream.WriteLine("   width: 100%;")
txtstream.WriteLine("}")
txtstream.WriteLine("input")
txtstream.WriteLine("{")
txtstream.WriteLine("   COLOR: black;")
txtstream.WriteLine("   BACKGROUND-COLOR: white;")
txtstream.WriteLine("   FONT-FAMILY: font-family: Cambria, serif;")
txtstream.WriteLine("   FONT-SIZE: 12px;")
txtstream.WriteLine("   text-align: left;")
txtstream.WriteLine("   display:table-cell;")
txtstream.WriteLine("   white-Space: nowrap;")
txtstream.WriteLine("}")
txtstream.WriteLine("h1 {")
txtstream.WriteLine("color: antiquewhite;")
txtstream.WriteLine("text-shadow: 1px 1px 1px black;")
txtstream.WriteLine("padding: 3px;")
txtstream.WriteLine("text-align: center;")
txtstream.WriteLine("box-shadow: inset 2px 2px 5px rgba(0,0,0,0.5), inset -2px -2px 5px rgba(255,255,255,0.5);")
txtstream.WriteLine("}")
txtstream.WriteLine("</style>")
```

3D

```
txtstream.WriteLine("<style type='text/css'>")
txtstream.WriteLine("body")
txtstream.WriteLine("{")
```

```
txtstream.WriteLine("    PADDING-RIGHT: 0px;")
txtstream.WriteLine("    PADDING-LEFT: 0px;")
txtstream.WriteLine("    PADDING-BOTTOM: 0px;")
txtstream.WriteLine("    MARGIN: 0px;")
txtstream.WriteLine("    COLOR: #333;")
txtstream.WriteLine("    PADDING-TOP: 0px;")
txtstream.WriteLine("    FONT-FAMILY: verdana, arial, helvetica, sans-serif;")
txtstream.WriteLine("}")
txtstream.WriteLine("table")
txtstream.WriteLine("{")
txtstream.WriteLine("    BORDER-RIGHT: #999999 3px solid;")
txtstream.WriteLine("    PADDING-RIGHT: 6px;")
txtstream.WriteLine("    PADDING-LEFT: 6px;")
txtstream.WriteLine("    FONT-WEIGHT: Bold;")
txtstream.WriteLine("    FONT-SIZE: 14px;")
txtstream.WriteLine("    PADDING-BOTTOM: 6px;")
txtstream.WriteLine("    COLOR: Peru;")
txtstream.WriteLine("    LINE-HEIGHT: 14px;")
txtstream.WriteLine("    PADDING-TOP: 6px;")
txtstream.WriteLine("    BORDER-BOTTOM: #999 1px solid;")
txtstream.WriteLine("    BACKGROUND-COLOR: #eeeeee;")
txtstream.WriteLine("    FONT-FAMILY: verdana, arial, helvetica, sans-serif;")
txtstream.WriteLine("    FONT-SIZE: 12px;")
txtstream.WriteLine("}")
txtstream.WriteLine("th")
txtstream.WriteLine("{")
txtstream.WriteLine("    BORDER-RIGHT: #999999 3px solid;")
txtstream.WriteLine("    PADDING-RIGHT: 6px;")
txtstream.WriteLine("    PADDING-LEFT: 6px;")
txtstream.WriteLine("    FONT-WEIGHT: Bold;")
txtstream.WriteLine("    FONT-SIZE: 14px;")
txtstream.WriteLine("    PADDING-BOTTOM: 6px;")
txtstream.WriteLine("    COLOR: darkred;")
```

```
txtstream.WriteLine("    LINE-HEIGHT: 14px;")
txtstream.WriteLine("    PADDING-TOP: 6px;")
txtstream.WriteLine("    BORDER-BOTTOM: #999 1px solid;")
txtstream.WriteLine("    BACKGROUND-COLOR: #eeeeee;")
txtstream.WriteLine("    FONT-FAMILY:font-family: Cambria, serif;")
txtstream.WriteLine("    FONT-SIZE: 12px;")
txtstream.WriteLine("    text-align: left;")
txtstream.WriteLine("    white-Space: nowrap;")
txtstream.WriteLine("}")
txtstream.WriteLine(".th")
txtstream.WriteLine("{")
txtstream.WriteLine("    BORDER-RIGHT: #999999 2px solid;")
txtstream.WriteLine("    PADDING-RIGHT: 6px;")
txtstream.WriteLine("    PADDING-LEFT: 6px;")
txtstream.WriteLine("    FONT-WEIGHT: Bold;")
txtstream.WriteLine("    PADDING-BOTTOM: 6px;")
txtstream.WriteLine("    COLOR: black;")
txtstream.WriteLine("    PADDING-TOP: 6px;")
txtstream.WriteLine("    BORDER-BOTTOM: #999 2px solid;")
txtstream.WriteLine("    BACKGROUND-COLOR: #eeeeee;")
txtstream.WriteLine("    FONT-FAMILY: font-family: Cambria, serif;")
txtstream.WriteLine("    FONT-SIZE: 10px;")
txtstream.WriteLine("    text-align: right;")
txtstream.WriteLine("    white-Space: nowrap;")
txtstream.WriteLine("}")
txtstream.WriteLine("td")
txtstream.WriteLine("{")
txtstream.WriteLine("    BORDER-RIGHT: #999999 3px solid;")
txtstream.WriteLine("    PADDING-RIGHT: 6px;")
txtstream.WriteLine("    PADDING-LEFT: 6px;")
txtstream.WriteLine("    FONT-WEIGHT: Normal;")
txtstream.WriteLine("    PADDING-BOTTOM: 6px;")
txtstream.WriteLine("    COLOR: navy;")
```

```
txtstream.WriteLine("    LINE-HEIGHT: 14px;")
txtstream.WriteLine("    PADDING-TOP: 6px;")
txtstream.WriteLine("    BORDER-BOTTOM: #999 1px solid;")
txtstream.WriteLine("    BACKGROUND-COLOR: #eeeeee;")
txtstream.WriteLine("    FONT-FAMILY: font-family: Cambria, serif;")
txtstream.WriteLine("    FONT-SIZE: 12px;")
txtstream.WriteLine("    text-align: left;")
txtstream.WriteLine("    white-Space: nowrap;")
txtstream.WriteLine("}")
txtstream.WriteLine("div")
txtstream.WriteLine("{")
txtstream.WriteLine("    BORDER-RIGHT: #999999 3px solid;")
txtstream.WriteLine("    PADDING-RIGHT: 6px;")
txtstream.WriteLine("    PADDING-LEFT: 6px;")
txtstream.WriteLine("    FONT-WEIGHT: Normal;")
txtstream.WriteLine("    PADDING-BOTTOM: 6px;")
txtstream.WriteLine("    COLOR: white;")
txtstream.WriteLine("    PADDING-TOP: 6px;")
txtstream.WriteLine("    BORDER-BOTTOM: #999 1px solid;")
txtstream.WriteLine("    BACKGROUND-COLOR: navy;")
txtstream.WriteLine("    FONT-FAMILY: font-family: Cambria, serif;")
txtstream.WriteLine("    FONT-SIZE: 10px;")
txtstream.WriteLine("    text-align: left;")
txtstream.WriteLine("    white-Space: nowrap;")
txtstream.WriteLine("}")
txtstream.WriteLine("span")
txtstream.WriteLine("{")
txtstream.WriteLine("    BORDER-RIGHT: #999999 3px solid;")
txtstream.WriteLine("    PADDING-RIGHT: 3px;")
txtstream.WriteLine("    PADDING-LEFT: 3px;")
txtstream.WriteLine("    FONT-WEIGHT: Normal;")
txtstream.WriteLine("    PADDING-BOTTOM: 3px;")
txtstream.WriteLine("    COLOR: white;")
```

```
txtstream.WriteLine("    PADDING-TOP: 3px;")
txtstream.WriteLine("    BORDER-BOTTOM: #999 1px solid;")
txtstream.WriteLine("    BACKGROUND-COLOR: navy;")
txtstream.WriteLine("    FONT-FAMILY: font-family: Cambria, serif;")
txtstream.WriteLine("    FONT-SIZE: 10px;")
txtstream.WriteLine("    text-align: left;")
txtstream.WriteLine("    white-Space: nowrap;")
txtstream.WriteLine("    display:inline-block;")
txtstream.WriteLine("    width: 100%;")
txtstream.WriteLine("}")
txtstream.WriteLine("textarea")
txtstream.WriteLine("{")
txtstream.WriteLine("    BORDER-RIGHT: #999999 3px solid;")
txtstream.WriteLine("    PADDING-RIGHT: 3px;")
txtstream.WriteLine("    PADDING-LEFT: 3px;")
txtstream.WriteLine("    FONT-WEIGHT: Normal;")
txtstream.WriteLine("    PADDING-BOTTOM: 3px;")
txtstream.WriteLine("    COLOR: white;")
txtstream.WriteLine("    PADDING-TOP: 3px;")
txtstream.WriteLine("    BORDER-BOTTOM: #999 1px solid;")
txtstream.WriteLine("    BACKGROUND-COLOR: navy;")
txtstream.WriteLine("    FONT-FAMILY: font-family: Cambria, serif;")
txtstream.WriteLine("    FONT-SIZE: 10px;")
txtstream.WriteLine("    text-align: left;")
txtstream.WriteLine("    white-Space: nowrap;")
txtstream.WriteLine("    width: 100%;")
txtstream.WriteLine("}")
txtstream.WriteLine("select")
txtstream.WriteLine("{")
txtstream.WriteLine("    BORDER-RIGHT: #999999 3px solid;")
txtstream.WriteLine("    PADDING-RIGHT: 6px;")
txtstream.WriteLine("    PADDING-LEFT: 6px;")
txtstream.WriteLine("    FONT-WEIGHT: Normal;")
```

```
txtstream.WriteLine("   PADDING-BOTTOM: 6px;")
txtstream.WriteLine("   COLOR: white;")
txtstream.WriteLine("   PADDING-TOP: 6px;")
txtstream.WriteLine("   BORDER-BOTTOM: #999 1px solid;")
txtstream.WriteLine("   BACKGROUND-COLOR: navy;")
txtstream.WriteLine("   FONT-FAMILY: font-family: Cambria, serif;")
txtstream.WriteLine("   FONT-SIZE: 10px;")
txtstream.WriteLine("   text-align: left;")
txtstream.WriteLine("   white-Space: nowrap;")
txtstream.WriteLine("   width: 100%;")
txtstream.WriteLine("}")
txtstream.WriteLine("input")
txtstream.WriteLine("{")
txtstream.WriteLine("   BORDER-RIGHT: #999999 3px solid;")
txtstream.WriteLine("   PADDING-RIGHT: 3px;")
txtstream.WriteLine("   PADDING-LEFT: 3px;")
txtstream.WriteLine("   FONT-WEIGHT: Bold;")
txtstream.WriteLine("   PADDING-BOTTOM: 3px;")
txtstream.WriteLine("   COLOR: white;")
txtstream.WriteLine("   PADDING-TOP: 3px;")
txtstream.WriteLine("   BORDER-BOTTOM: #999 1px solid;")
txtstream.WriteLine("   BACKGROUND-COLOR: navy;")
txtstream.WriteLine("   FONT-FAMILY: font-family: Cambria, serif;")
txtstream.WriteLine("   FONT-SIZE: 12px;")
txtstream.WriteLine("   text-align: left;")
txtstream.WriteLine("   display:table-cell;")
txtstream.WriteLine("   white-Space: nowrap;")
txtstream.WriteLine("   width: 100%;")
txtstream.WriteLine("}")
txtstream.WriteLine("h1 {")
txtstream.WriteLine("color: antiquewhite;")
txtstream.WriteLine("text-shadow: 1px 1px 1px black;")
txtstream.WriteLine("padding: 3px;")
```

```
txtstream.WriteLine("text-align: center;")
txtstream.WriteLine("box-shadow: inset 2px 2px 5px rgba(0,0,0,0.5), inset -
2px -2px 5px rgba(255,255,255,0.5);")
txtstream.WriteLine("}")
txtstream.WriteLine("</style>")
```

SHADOW BOX

```
txtstream.WriteLine("<style type='text/css'>")
txtstream.WriteLine("body")
txtstream.WriteLine("{")
txtstream.WriteLine("  PADDING-RIGHT: 0px;")
txtstream.WriteLine("  PADDING-LEFT: 0px;")
txtstream.WriteLine("  PADDING-BOTTOM: 0px;")
txtstream.WriteLine("  MARGIN: 0px;")
txtstream.WriteLine("  COLOR: #333;")
txtstream.WriteLine("  PADDING-TOP: 0px;")
txtstream.WriteLine("  FONT-FAMILY: verdana, arial, helvetica, sans-serif;")
txtstream.WriteLine("}")
txtstream.WriteLine("table")
txtstream.WriteLine("{")
txtstream.WriteLine("  BORDER-RIGHT: #999999 1px solid;")
txtstream.WriteLine("  PADDING-RIGHT: 1px;")
txtstream.WriteLine("  PADDING-LEFT: 1px;")
txtstream.WriteLine("  PADDING-BOTTOM: 1px;")
txtstream.WriteLine("  LINE-HEIGHT: 8px;")
txtstream.WriteLine("  PADDING-TOP: 1px;")
txtstream.WriteLine("  BORDER-BOTTOM: #999 1px solid;")
txtstream.WriteLine("  BACKGROUND-COLOR: #eeeeee;")
txtstream.WriteLine("
filter:progid:DXImageTransform.Microsoft.Shadow(color='silver',     Direction=135,
Strength=16")
txtstream.WriteLine("}")
```

```
txtstream.WriteLine("th")
txtstream.WriteLine("{")
txtstream.WriteLine("    BORDER-RIGHT: #999999 3px solid;")
txtstream.WriteLine("    PADDING-RIGHT: 6px;")
txtstream.WriteLine("    PADDING-LEFT: 6px;")
txtstream.WriteLine("    FONT-WEIGHT: Bold;")
txtstream.WriteLine("    FONT-SIZE: 14px;")
txtstream.WriteLine("    PADDING-BOTTOM: 6px;")
txtstream.WriteLine("    COLOR: darkred;")
txtstream.WriteLine("    LINE-HEIGHT: 14px;")
txtstream.WriteLine("    PADDING-TOP: 6px;")
txtstream.WriteLine("    BORDER-BOTTOM: #999 1px solid;")
txtstream.WriteLine("    BACKGROUND-COLOR: #eeeeee;")
txtstream.WriteLine("    FONT-FAMILY: font-family: Cambria, serif;")
txtstream.WriteLine("    FONT-SIZE: 12px;")
txtstream.WriteLine("    text-align: left;")
txtstream.WriteLine("    white-Space: nowrap;")
txtstream.WriteLine("}")
txtstream.WriteLine(".th")
txtstream.WriteLine("{")
txtstream.WriteLine("    BORDER-RIGHT: #999999 2px solid;")
txtstream.WriteLine("    PADDING-RIGHT: 6px;")
txtstream.WriteLine("    PADDING-LEFT: 6px;")
txtstream.WriteLine("    FONT-WEIGHT: Bold;")
txtstream.WriteLine("    PADDING-BOTTOM: 6px;")
txtstream.WriteLine("    COLOR: black;")
txtstream.WriteLine("    PADDING-TOP: 6px;")
txtstream.WriteLine("    BORDER-BOTTOM: #999 2px solid;")
txtstream.WriteLine("    BACKGROUND-COLOR: #eeeeee;")
txtstream.WriteLine("    FONT-FAMILY: font-family: Cambria, serif;")
txtstream.WriteLine("    FONT-SIZE: 10px;")
txtstream.WriteLine("    text-align: right;")
txtstream.WriteLine("    white-Space: nowrap;")
```

```
txtstream.WriteLine("}")
txtstream.WriteLine("td")
txtstream.WriteLine("{")
txtstream.WriteLine("   BORDER-RIGHT: #999999 3px solid;")
txtstream.WriteLine("   PADDING-RIGHT: 6px;")
txtstream.WriteLine("   PADDING-LEFT: 6px;")
txtstream.WriteLine("   FONT-WEIGHT: Normal;")
txtstream.WriteLine("   PADDING-BOTTOM: 6px;")
txtstream.WriteLine("   COLOR: navy;")
txtstream.WriteLine("   LINE-HEIGHT: 14px;")
txtstream.WriteLine("   PADDING-TOP: 6px;")
txtstream.WriteLine("   BORDER-BOTTOM: #999 1px solid;")
txtstream.WriteLine("   BACKGROUND-COLOR: #eeeeee;")
txtstream.WriteLine("   FONT-FAMILY: font-family: Cambria, serif;")
txtstream.WriteLine("   FONT-SIZE: 12px;")
txtstream.WriteLine("   text-align: left;")
txtstream.WriteLine("   white-Space: nowrap;")
txtstream.WriteLine("}")
txtstream.WriteLine("div")
txtstream.WriteLine("{")
txtstream.WriteLine("   BORDER-RIGHT: #999999 3px solid;")
txtstream.WriteLine("   PADDING-RIGHT: 6px;")
txtstream.WriteLine("   PADDING-LEFT: 6px;")
txtstream.WriteLine("   FONT-WEIGHT: Normal;")
txtstream.WriteLine("   PADDING-BOTTOM: 6px;")
txtstream.WriteLine("   COLOR: white;")
txtstream.WriteLine("   PADDING-TOP: 6px;")
txtstream.WriteLine("   BORDER-BOTTOM: #999 1px solid;")
txtstream.WriteLine("   BACKGROUND-COLOR: navy;")
txtstream.WriteLine("   FONT-FAMILY: font-family: Cambria, serif;")
txtstream.WriteLine("   FONT-SIZE: 10px;")
txtstream.WriteLine("   text-align: left;")
txtstream.WriteLine("   white-Space: nowrap;")
```

```
txtstream.WriteLine("}")
txtstream.WriteLine("span")
txtstream.WriteLine("{")
txtstream.WriteLine("    BORDER-RIGHT: #999999 3px solid;")
txtstream.WriteLine("    PADDING-RIGHT: 3px;")
txtstream.WriteLine("    PADDING-LEFT: 3px;")
txtstream.WriteLine("    FONT-WEIGHT: Normal;")
txtstream.WriteLine("    PADDING-BOTTOM: 3px;")
txtstream.WriteLine("    COLOR: white;")
txtstream.WriteLine("    PADDING-TOP: 3px;")
txtstream.WriteLine("    BORDER-BOTTOM: #999 1px solid;")
txtstream.WriteLine("    BACKGROUND-COLOR: navy;")
txtstream.WriteLine("    FONT-FAMILY: font-family: Cambria, serif;")
txtstream.WriteLine("    FONT-SIZE: 10px;")
txtstream.WriteLine("    text-align: left;")
txtstream.WriteLine("    white-Space: nowrap;")
txtstream.WriteLine("    display: inline-block;")
txtstream.WriteLine("    width: 100%;")
txtstream.WriteLine("}")
txtstream.WriteLine("textarea")
txtstream.WriteLine("{")
txtstream.WriteLine("    BORDER-RIGHT: #999999 3px solid;")
txtstream.WriteLine("    PADDING-RIGHT: 3px;")
txtstream.WriteLine("    PADDING-LEFT: 3px;")
txtstream.WriteLine("    FONT-WEIGHT: Normal;")
txtstream.WriteLine("    PADDING-BOTTOM: 3px;")
txtstream.WriteLine("    COLOR: white;")
txtstream.WriteLine("    PADDING-TOP: 3px;")
txtstream.WriteLine("    BORDER-BOTTOM: #999 1px solid;")
txtstream.WriteLine("    BACKGROUND-COLOR: navy;")
txtstream.WriteLine("    FONT-FAMILY: font-family: Cambria, serif;")
txtstream.WriteLine("    FONT-SIZE: 10px;")
txtstream.WriteLine("    text-align: left;")
```

```
txtstream.WriteLine("    white-Space: nowrap;")
txtstream.WriteLine("    width: 100%;")
txtstream.WriteLine("}")
txtstream.WriteLine("select")
txtstream.WriteLine("{")
txtstream.WriteLine("    BORDER-RIGHT: #999999 3px solid;")
txtstream.WriteLine("    PADDING-RIGHT: 6px;")
txtstream.WriteLine("    PADDING-LEFT: 6px;")
txtstream.WriteLine("    FONT-WEIGHT: Normal;")
txtstream.WriteLine("    PADDING-BOTTOM: 6px;")
txtstream.WriteLine("    COLOR: white;")
txtstream.WriteLine("    PADDING-TOP: 6px;")
txtstream.WriteLine("    BORDER-BOTTOM: #999 1px solid;")
txtstream.WriteLine("    BACKGROUND-COLOR: navy;")
txtstream.WriteLine("    FONT-FAMILY: font-family: Cambria, serif;")
txtstream.WriteLine("    FONT-SIZE: 10px;")
txtstream.WriteLine("    text-align: left;")
txtstream.WriteLine("    white-Space: nowrap;")
txtstream.WriteLine("    width: 100%;")
txtstream.WriteLine("}")
txtstream.WriteLine("input")
txtstream.WriteLine("{")
txtstream.WriteLine("    BORDER-RIGHT: #999999 3px solid;")
txtstream.WriteLine("    PADDING-RIGHT: 3px;")
txtstream.WriteLine("    PADDING-LEFT: 3px;")
txtstream.WriteLine("    FONT-WEIGHT: Bold;")
txtstream.WriteLine("    PADDING-BOTTOM: 3px;")
txtstream.WriteLine("    COLOR: white;")
txtstream.WriteLine("    PADDING-TOP: 3px;")
txtstream.WriteLine("    BORDER-BOTTOM: #999 1px solid;")
txtstream.WriteLine("    BACKGROUND-COLOR: navy;")
txtstream.WriteLine("    FONT-FAMILY: font-family: Cambria, serif;")
txtstream.WriteLine("    FONT-SIZE: 12px;")
```

```
txtstream.WriteLine("    text-align: left;")
txtstream.WriteLine("    display: table-cell;")
txtstream.WriteLine("    white-Space: nowrap;")
txtstream.WriteLine("    width: 100%;")
txtstream.WriteLine("}")
txtstream.WriteLine("h1 {")
txtstream.WriteLine("color: antiquewhite;")
txtstream.WriteLine("text-shadow: 1px 1px 1px black;")
txtstream.WriteLine("padding: 3px;")
txtstream.WriteLine("text-align: center;")
txtstream.WriteLine("box-shadow: inset 2px 2px 5px rgba(0,0,0,0.5), inset -2px -2px 5px rgba(255,255,255,0.5);")
txtstream.WriteLine("}")
txtstream.WriteLine("</style>")
```

Appendix B

The GetValue routine

Chapter Epigraph uses a quote or verse to
introduce the chapter and set the stage.
—Attribute the quote

SPECIFICALLY PLACED THIS HERE BECAUSE THE ROUTE TAKES UP AROUND 30 OF THIS BOOK AND I WANTED TO REPLACE IT WITH SOME STYLESHEET BEAUTIFICATION OF THE EXAMPLES.

```
Function GetValue(ByVal Name, ByVal obj)

    Dim tempstr, pos, pName
    pName = Name
    tempstr = obj.GetObjectText_
    Name = Name + " = "
    pos = InStr(tempstr, Name)
    if pos Then
        pos = pos + Len(Name)
```

```
      tempstr = Mid(tempstr, pos, Len(tempstr))
      pos = InStr(tempstr, ";")
      tempstr = Mid(tempstr, 1, pos - 1)
      tempstr = Replace(tempstr, Chr(34), "")
      tempstr = Replace(tempstr, "{", "")
      tempstr = Replace(tempstr, "}", "")
      tempstr = Trim(tempstr)
      if obj.Properties_(pName).CIMType = 101 Then
        tempstr = Mid(tempstr, 5, 2) + "/" + _
        Mid(tempstr, 7, 2) + "/" + _
        Mid(tempstr, 1, 4) + " " + _
        Mid(tempstr, 9, 2) + ":" + _
        Mid(tempstr, 11, 2) + ":" + _
        Mid(tempstr, 13, 2)
      End If
    GetValue = tempstr
    Else
     GetValue = ""
    End If

End Function
```

www.ingramcontent.com/pod-product-compliance
Lightning Source LLC
Chambersburg PA
CBHW070835070326
40690CB00009B/1550